History of
ART

This edition published by Barnes & Noble Inc.,
by arrangement with Parragon Publishing

2005 Barnes & Noble Books

M 10 9 8 7 6 5 4 3 2 1

ISBN 0-7607-6796-3

Printed and bound in Indonesia

Acknowledgments

This book has been made possible by four authors: Lucinda Hawksley, Antonia
Cunningham, Laura Payne, and Kirsten Bradbury. They have all written extensively on a
variety of subjects in the art world, including several titles in the Essential Art series of
books. They are currently living and working in or around London.

Additional and updated text provided by Image Select International, with special thanks to
Joanna Nadine Roberts and Peter A.F. Goldberg.

While every endeavor has been made to ensure the accuracy of the reproduction of the
images in this book, we would be grateful to receive any comments or suggestions for
inclusion in future reprints. The author and publishers have made every reasonable effort to
contact all copyright holders. Any errors that may have occurred are inadvertent and
anyone who for any reason has not been contacted is invited to write to the publishers so
that full acknowledgement may be made in subsequent editions of this work.

With thanks to Image Select for sourcing the pictures in this book.

The right of Kirsten Bradbury, Antonia Cunningham,
Lucinda Hawksley and Laura Payne to be identified as the
author of this work has been asserted in accordance with
Section 77 of the Copyright, Designs and Patents Act of 1988.

History of
ART

BARNES & NOBLE BOOKS
NEW YORK

CONTENTS

CONTENTS

Contents

Contents

Contents

History of Art introduces a new, chronological way of looking at the major movements in the Western art world over the last two thousand years. It is the only book to examine the roots of art in prehistory and provide seminal examples of work from 240 of the leading artists in the context of their school, period, vision and technique. For example, only in this book is it possible to compare a major work by Salvador Dalí to the work of contemporaries such as Pablo Picasso and René Magritte. Each artist is represented by a full-color plate of an important work, and this is accompanied by text explaining their impact on and relevance to the development of art, and a brief history of the artist's life. Glossaries of artistic movements and technical terms are included at the end of the book. This book allows the reader to see the development of art chronologically within each specific movement, and in addition provides a sourcebook for some of the most famous images in the Western world.

LASCAUX CAVE PAINTINGS

BISON

Altamira Cave, Santillana de Mar. Celimage.sa/Lessing Archive

THE painted ceiling of the Altamira Cave is probably the most famous Paleolithic wall painting. The painted area measures approximately 650 ft in length and 30 ft in width.

The Altamira Cave was discovered in 1869 by Marcelino de Santuola, and in 1879, the first paintings were discovered. Their surprising quality and exceptionally well-preserved state is extraordinary. The cave offers clear evidence of Paleolithic culture in Southern Europe.

On the ceiling of the main hall there are many splendid, multi-colored paintings. They are unique for the richness of their depictions of bison, horse, red deer, and boar, and they are remarkably lifelike. The paintings have an unusually clear dynamic; they are teeming with movement, and the unevenness of the stone surface lends a three-dimensional aspect to the subjects.

The ceiling painting is of 15 large bison interspersed with a few other animals including a horse.

The bison are richly textured, painted in a reddish ocher with strong black outlines. Bison were hunted primarily for the food they provided, but many other useful commodities like skin, bones, and fur could be extracted from the remains.

Altamira Cave is known as the Sistine Chapel of Paleolithic art, and access to the cave is restricted today to prevent damage to the paintings.

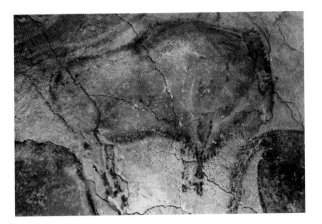

PALACE OF MINOS, KNOSSOS, CRETE

FRESCO OF A TOREADOR

National Archeological Museum, Athens. Celimage.sa/Lessing Archive

THE Minoan civilization flourished from c.3000–1100 BC. The Palace of Minos at Knossos, in Crete, was one of three built by the early Minoans. It was ruined, along with the palaces of Phaistos and Malia, when an earthquake devastated the entire area in c.1700 BC. The palaces were rebuilt but another earthquake, in c.1450 BC, destroyed them a second time. After the collapse of the Minoan civilization at about the same time, the area was settled by the Myceneans.

The Palace of Minos was so named because it is believed to have been the home of the legendary King Minos, son of Zeus and Europa. In Greek mythology the palace also housed the labyrinth of the Minotaur—a creature with the head of a bull and the body of a man, which required human flesh for sustenance. According to one story, the sea god Poseidon took revenge on Minos for failing to sacrifice a white bull in his honor by causing his wife Pasiphaë to give birth to the Minotaur.

This fresco, which was excavated at the palace, appears to be of a bullfight—although no weapons are visible. The association with the Minotaur may explain the subject matter of the fresco.

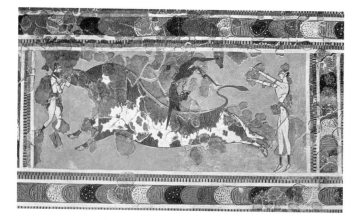

EGYPTIAN ART

DEATH MASK OF TUTANKHAMUN

Egyptian National Museum, Cairo. Celimage.sa/Lessing Archive

ANCIENT Egypt has given the world some of its most spectacular art treasures, and the death mask of Tutankhamun is perhaps the most famous. Throughout the 3,000 years of Pharaonic rule, there were 31 dynasties. Tutankhamun was a relatively minor boy-king, who ruled for nine years during the era of the New Kingdom (1575–1087 BC).

The grave goods of Tutankhamun have assumed enormous importance today because his tomb was found intact, whereas those of the greater Pharaohs were robbed many centuries ago. The treasures of Tutankhamun's grave included golden chariots, life-size statues, gems, precious metals, clothing, and mummy cases. It is impossible to speculate on the wealth of treasure that was once contained in tombs of the more important Pharaohs.

Created from gold and precious stones, including lapis lazuli, the death mask is breathtaking. The mask has symbolic significance: Tutankhamun's beard and headcloth (*nemes*) were symbols of his royalty; the cobra on his forehead was protective, its role being to spit poison at enemies of the Pharaoh; lapis lazuli was also believed to have powers of protection.

Ancient Art

GREEK SCULPTURE

THE SUPPLICANT BARBERINI

Louvre, Paris. Celimage.sa/Lessing Archive

PORTRAIT sculpture was little known in Greece before the seventh century BC, when it became a recognizable and respected art form. The earliest Greek sculptures of people were evocative of the art of ancient Egypt: there are many *kouros* (youths) and *kore* (young women) dating from around 650 BC which emulate Egyptian sculpture in their use of stylized eyes and static poses, and in their rigid portrayal of clothing.

However, Greek sculpture differed in one important respect—it was freestanding. Whereas Egyptian sculpture tended to remain fixed within a block of stone, in Greek sculpture any dispensable stone was cut away, creating space between the legs and between the arms and body; this technique allowed greater freedom of expression on the part of the sculptor and widened the range of subjects that were depicted.

The Supplicant Barberini dates from c.400 BC. In comparison to the stiff, awkward *kouros* of an earlier era, it heralds an entirely new approach to marble portraiture. The face is far from stylized, depicting a real likeness, if not of Barberini then of the face of the sculptor's model. The limbs are no longer static, and the drapery hangs in folds as real material would, in sharp contrast to the stiff, A-line robes of early *kore*.

ETRUSCAN ART

ETRUSCAN AMPHORA

Louvre, Paris. Celimage.sa/Lessing Archive

ETRUSCAN civilization flourished in western Italy from c.900–c.100 BC. Ancient Etruria encompassed modern Tuscany and parts of Umbria, and was roughly equivalent to the area between the rivers Arno and Tiber south of Florence, north of Rome and west of the Apennines.

Etruscan art was influenced by the Asian, Greek, and Roman civilizations. The technique of decorating pottery with "red-figure painting" had been initiated in Etruria during the Greek period and remained in common practice during Roman times. Before this, the common decorative method had been "black-figure painting," in which artists painted their work in black pigment onto a base of red clay. In Greek pottery, red-figure painting was created by sketching the outline of the subject and then painting the background in black, leaving the design to show through in the color of the clay. Etruscan artists painted the entire surface in black and then painted over the top of this in a terracotta-colored pigment.

The pottery vase shown here probably dates from the early Roman occupation of Etruria, although it could be from the late Greek era. It depicts a maritime scene, with fantastical sea creatures parading along the surface of the vase.

POMPEIIAN FRESCO

THE BAKER AND HIS WIFE

National Archeological Museum, Naples. Celimage.sa/Lessing Archive

POMPEII was an ancient Roman country town near Naples in western Italy. It was destroyed when Mount Vesuvius erupted in AD 79. Pompeii and its inhabitants were suffocated beneath the falling ash, although the town was perfectly preserved for centuries under successive layers of mud and vegetation.

In 1748 archeologists began reclaiming Pompeii. The town appears to have been moderately wealthy and every house, from the most palatial to the most lowly, was decorated with wall paintings. Mosaics were also common.

Artwork found in Pompeii, Herculaneum, and Stabiae is known as Campanian Art, and is representative of all southern Italian painting at the time. As Pompeii was then under Roman rule it is also indicative of Roman art at this time, which had been heavily influenced by earlier Greek art.

This particular work was painted onto a wall adjacent to the baker's house, and many believe that it depicts the baker, Paquius Proculus, and his wife. Others contend that the man may be a wealthy lawyer named Terentius Neus. The couple appear to be upper class; the woman is elegantly dressed and coiffed, while he sports a white toga and carries a scroll.

BASILICA DI SAN MARCO, VENICE

BRONZE HORSES (DETAIL)

San Marco, Venice. Celimage.sa/Lessing Archive

THE four bronze horses now seen at the Basilica di San Marco in Venice were originally made for the Hippodrome in Constantinople (now Istanbul), which was then under Roman occupation. The Hippodrome, the largest in the ancient world, could seat 60,000 spectators. A low wall ran round much of the stadium and this was decorated with dozens of monuments, including the bronze horses. In 1204, during the crusades, the horses were stolen by Christian knights and taken to Venice.

For many years the four horses stood on the Loggia dei Cavalli (part of the basilica's façade), from where visitors can look out over St Mark's Square. Today the horses on the loggia are replicas; the originals were removed in 1979, in the cause of their preservation, and can now be seen inside the cathedral's museum. For centuries during medieval times these horses symbolized the power and prestige of the Venetian Republic; they were probably made during the second century AD. Their sculptor is generally assumed to have been Roman. The material used was bronze, an alloy of copper and tin—the bronze used here was very rich in copper—and the bronze was then gilded.

BURIAL NICHES WITH FRESCO

CHRIST, RULER OF THE WORLD (PANTOCRATOR)

Catacombs of Saint Calxtus, Rome. Celimage.sa/Lessing Archive

LYING outside the walls of the ancient city of Rome, these catacombs are probably the best preserved examples of early Christian art. The early converts to the religion decorated the resting-places of their dead in a similar manner to the Egyptians and Etruscans by painting frescoes directly onto walls built of untreated chalky subsoil, so it is remarkable that any of their delicate work has survived.

This fragile sepulchre art uses mostly simplistic color and line, with solid figures placed in an illusionistic setting. To avoid possible confrontation with existing authorities, traditional Classical and pagan motifs were adapted to express early Christian stories and concepts, although manipulation of the imagery was so subtle that it was only truly understood by cult members who had been initiated into the new church rituals.

This picture shows *Christ, Ruler of the World (Pantocrator)* from the Catacombs of Saint Calxtus, in Rome. The catacombs are some of the earliest examples of Western Christian art, dating from the first and second centuries AD.

MOSAICS FROM RAVENNA

CHRIST SEPARATES THE SHEEP FROM THE GOATS

Sant'Apollinare Nuovo, Ravenna. Celimage.sa/Lessing Archive

BYZANTINE art saw the fusion of pagan and Eastern iconography with early Christian images to create a highly influential artistic language of spiritual religiosity. The idealist philosophy of mystical knowledge—that man, through initiation, could transcend the world of appearances and gain admission to the spiritual plane—saw images of reality transformed into esoteric symbols.

These stunning Christian mosaics from Ravenna in Italy are among the earliest examples of the resplendent art produced by the Byzantine Empire between AD 330 and 1453. During the glorious "Golden Ages" of Byzantine art—between the sixth and seventh centuries and from the ninth to the twelfth century—wall and panel paintings, illuminated manuscripts, and mosaics were all subjected to the same lavish treatment, until realism of form returned with the early Renaissance and the humanist movement in the fifteenth century.

Byzantine art was concerned with symmetry and ornamentation rather than an imitation of life, reflecting the superior dimensions of an ideal universe. Images are seen suspended, as if in flight, against abstract gold backgrounds. Notions of horizon, expressive movement, and rational perspective, which had been explored by the Greeks in the half-profile or three-quarter view, were replaced with flat, full-frontal figures, as in this section of mosaic frieze from the church of Sant'Apollinare Nuovo.

Byzantine Art

THE LINDISFARNE GOSPELS

SAINT JOHN THE EVANGELIST

British Library, London. Courtesy of the Ann Ronan Picture Library

IRISH missionary Saint Aidan (600–651) arrived in Northumbria in 635 from the Hebridean island of Iona. He founded a monastery at Lindisfarne, where the Lindisfarne Gospels were created by Irish monks. Their spectacular illuminations and jewel-encrusted binding reflect the importance of God's word, spoken through the Bible.

According to notes added to the Lindisfarne Gospels in c. 950, the creator of the binding was a bishop of Lindisfarne, Aethelwald. Another bishop, Eadfrith, was the scribe and he is also presumed to be the artist of the illuminated pictures. The translation of the text (from Latin into English) was undertaken by a priest of Lindisfarne, Aldred. In 875 Viking raids caused the monks to flee Lindisfarne, taking the gospels with them.

This type of illumination is in the Hiberno-Saxon style, which encompasses elements of pagan art, such as Celtic design, as well as influences from elsewhere in Europe. The Celtic element is apparent in the intricate design of the goldwork. This facsimile page shows Celtic influence, in the style of figurative portrayal, as well as in the patterns and borders.

THE APOCALYPSE OF BEATUS

NOAH TAKING THE OLIVE TWIG FROM THE DOVE'S BEAK

Capitular de Osma Archive, Soria. Celimage.sa/Lessing Archive

BEATUS was an abbot who lived in Liébana, northern Spain. In c. 776 he wrote his masterpiece, a manuscript describing the apocalypse—the biblical end of the world. The theme was a common one for scholars and religious leaders. Beatus's *Apocalypse* was an extremely popular version of the story, which was reproduced by monastic communities for their own use. His work was passed down through generations of scholars and there are now 25 surviving copies, produced between the tenth and thirteenth centuries. These range in size from large-format manuscripts, obviously created for use in churches and cathedrals, to small illuminated manuscripts for personal use.

The monks who painted illuminated manuscripts at this time were influenced by several artistic styles, most prominently Byzantine art, but also Celtic, Germanic, and early Christian art. This version of Beatus's *Apocalypse* can still be seen in Soria, in central Spain, housed in the Archivo Capitular de Osma, in the village of El Burgo de Osma.

THE BOOK OF KELLS

SAINT MATTHEW

Trinity College, Dublin. Courtesy of the Ann Ronan Picture Library

THE Book of Kells contains the four gospels in Latin, and was created by Irish monks living at Iona, an island in Scotland's Inner Hebrides. The pages are made of vellum and decorated with richly colored dyes, some imported from the Middle East. Monks created such works as a sign of their obedience and devotion to God, believing that the word of God should only be recorded within scenes of beauty.

Iona was a place of great spirituality and learning, closely allied to Mayo Abbey in Ireland, another site of great religious importance. Saint Columba, a sixth-century Irish missionary and priest, founded the monastery on Iona in c. 563, remaining there for the rest of his life. After his death (in 597), the monastery continued to thrive until the arrival of the first Viking marauders from Scandinavia in 804–07.

The Viking invasions caused the monks to flee to Kells in Ireland, leaving the Book of Kells unfinished. Nonetheless, it is one of the most spectacular surviving examples of illuminated medieval manuscripts.

LAVANTTAL MANUSCRIPT

EMPEROR CHARLEMAGNE AND HIS WIFE

Abbey Library, St Paul im Lavanttal. Celimage.sa/Lessing Archive

CHARLEMAGNE, or Charles the Great, was born in 742 in Northern Europe. "By the sword and the cross," he became master of Western Europe. His childhood was consumed by the responsibility of preparing himself as heir to his father, King Pepin. In 768, just before his death, the king divided his lands between his two sons.

This early medieval manuscript illustration from the ninth century features Charlemagne and his wife. The document's age is clearly visible in the weathered creases along its surface and the browning of the parchment itself. Yet the colors used to depict the royal couple have retained their strength throughout the image. Dark reds and oranges have been used to detail the characters and the archways stretching above them.

This particular work is a detail from an illuminated manuscript. Manuscripts were the books that were produced manually between the fifth and sixteenth centuries. They were the main source of visual recording in Europe until around the fifth century, when the codex was used for long texts, concurrently with the Christianization of Europe.

THE BAYEUX TAPESTRY

SCENE FROM THE BAYEUX TAPESTRY

Courtesy of the Ann Ronan Picture Library

THE Bayeux Tapestry depicts events that happened in the years 1065–66, leading up to the Norman Conquest of England. It constitutes a vitally important historical record and is extremely valuable for the information it reveals about military tactics and equipment of the time. The scenes were embroidered, in two types of wool and eight different colors, onto a bare strip of linen and accompanied by a Latin text.

In fact, the Bayeux Tapestry is a fine example of medieval English embroidery, not a tapestry at all, and is thought to have been made in Canterbury, England. Tapestry is a medium in which the pattern is an integral part of the cloth, incorporated into the material as it is woven.

The story of William the Conqueror's defeat of the English King Harold in 1066 is depicted in 79 scenes, which span over 70 m (230 ft) in length and 50 cm (19.5 in) in height. The tapestry was probably commissioned by William's half-brother, Bishop Odo of Bayeux.

For many centuries the Bayeux Tapestry was apparently forgotten. It was not until the eighteenth century that it was rediscovered, by two French archeologists. It is now on display in Bayeux, Normandy.

Early Medieval

PIETRO CAVALLINI (C.1250–C.1330)

THE LAST JUDGMENT (DETAIL)

Santa Cecilia in Trastevere, Rome. Celimage.sa/Lessing Archive

PIETRO Cavallini was an Italian fresco painter and designer of mosaics who spent most of his life in Rome. His dates of birth and death are unclear but he is known to have been artistically active between 1273 and 1308.

Cavallini was remarkable for his radical move away from the accepted Byzantine style of art. Although his work retained certain Byzantine elements, he also looked to other styles of art, in particular to the art of antiquity as well as more natural European influences. As a result, his work is imbued with a simplicity (although not to its detriment) unusual for its era.

Little of his work survives but his impressive fresco technique can be seen in *The Last Judgment*, which was painted for the church of Santa Cecilia in Trastevere in Rome. His move away from the Byzantine style is apparent in the pale colors he employed. His work is also notable for the individuality of the faces personifying Christ and his Apostles, painted to reflect each man's character and not to an archetypal ideal. A series of Cavallini's mosaics chronicling *The Life of the Virgin* (1291) can still be seen in Santa Maria in Trastevere, also in Rome.

Early Medieval

23

CIMABUE (C.1240–1302)

SANTA TRINITÀ MADONNA

Uffizi Gallery, Florence. Celimage.sa/Lessing Archive

CENNI di Peppi, known as Cimabue, is traditionally believed to have been Giotto's (1267–1337) teacher and is credited with preparing the ground for the naturalism of Giotto's revolutionary style. By comparison with the latter's work, Cimabue's painting is flat and decorative, in keeping with the traditional Byzantine style, although it exhibited a naturalism and intensity that was unusual at the time. Cimabue's style may have sprung out of a visit to Rome in 1272, where mural painters and mosaicists were beginning to create naturalistic effects.

In the *Santa Trinità Madonna* the Virgin is enthroned with Christ in her arms and surrounded by angels. The painting, acknowledged as Cimabue's masterpiece, was originally executed for Santa Trinità Church in Florence, and shows a sweetness and dignity that is unusual in Byzantine painting.

The faces of the angels, although similar, are expressive and seem to show an awareness of one another. Moreover, although Cimabue "stacks" the angels on either side of the throne, with no real suggestion of depth, his architectural treatment of the throne shows an attempt to create a realistic, three-dimensional space—a new concept in art that was to be taken up with even greater effect by Giotto.

Gothic Medieval

GIOTTO DI BONDONE (1267–1337)

THE ANNUNCIATION TO SAINT ANNE, MOTHER OF THE VIRGIN

Scrovegni Chapel, Padua. Celimage.sa/Lessing Archive

THE Florentine painter Giotto is one of the most important artists in the history of Western art. A friend of the Italian poet Dante Alighieri (1265–1321) and reputed to be a pupil of Cimabue, he was the first artist of the medieval period to approach the human figure as a sculptural mass inhabiting its own space. He was also responsible for breaking with the saccharine sweetness found in the work of many earlier medieval artists. His work displays a complex language of communication, and for the first time portrays the real emotions of its subjects.

When Giotto died in 1337, there was no one to take up his mantle of greatness. It was not until Masaccio (1401–c.1428) that a suitable successor to his talents, innovation, and skill appeared.

In the Scrovegni Chapel at Padua (painted 1304–07), Giotto's fresco, *The Annunciation to Saint Anne*, shows Saint Anne being told by an angel that she will conceive a child, despite having been barren.

DUCCIO DI BUONINSEGNA (C.1255–1318)

MAESTÀ

Museo dell'Opera Metropolitana, Siena. Celimage.sa/Scala Archives

DUCCIO, a near-contemporary of Cimabue, hailed from Siena, a city that had a great cultural rivalry with its close neighbor Florence, although the towns followed different artistic paths. As Italian art moved away from the Byzantine style of the Middle Ages, the Sienese school turned toward a decorative, almost courtly art, based on Byzantine traditions but marked by its use of color and attention to detail.

In his early work Duccio was very close to Cimabue in style, concentrating on pattern with very little attempt at depth. His influence, however, was more far-reaching than that of Cimabue, and was to have an effect on the next 200 years of Sienese painting. The *Maestà* (meaning "majesty"), commissioned in 1308, was installed in Siena Cathedral in 1311, and marked the culmination of Duccio's success. It was one of the largest panel paintings ever made in Italy.

The central panel portrays the Madonna and Child with saints. Around them and on the back are smaller scenes showing dramatic narratives from the life of Christ. In the painting Duccio shows a greater degree of naturalism than his contemporaries, especially in the formation of the drapery, and a new concern for space and perspective, although the figures are delicate and the traditional gold background serves to flatten the space.

ANDREA PISANO (C.1290–1348)

BAPTISM OF CHRIST BY JOHN THE BAPTIST

The Baptistry Doors, the Duomo, Florence. Celimage.sa/Scala Archives

ANDREA Pisano was born near Pisa. According to art historian Vasari (1511–74), he went to Florence to work on the west façade of the Duomo, which was designed by his friend Giotto. In 1330 he received a further commission to make a pair of bronze doors for the Baptistry in Florence. Pisano originally designed the East Doors but these were later moved to the south entrance to make way for Ghiberti's *Gates of Paradise* (1425–59).

The doors were hung in 1336, and in 1340, three years after Giotto's death, Pisano became architect of the Duomo. In 1347 he was appointed Master of Works at Orvieto Cathedral.

Pisano's theme for the design of the Baptistry doors was the life of Saint John the Baptist. Set in a quatrefoil pierced by a square—a French decorative motif—20 bronze relief panels run across both doors, from left to right, telling the story of John's birth, ministry, and death. Pisano's style—with sculpted, three-dimensional figures and an overall design aimed at creating drama—is profoundly influenced by that of Giotto. This panel shows the baptism of Christ by John the Baptist.

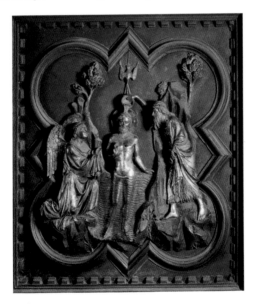

AMBROGIO LORENZETTI (C.1313–1348)

THE EFFECTS OF GOOD GOVERNMENT

Palazzo Pubblico, Siena. Celimage.sa/Scala Archives

AMBROGIO Lorenzetti was a Sienese painter and the younger brother of the artist Pietro (c.1280–1348), who may have been his teacher. He was familiar with the work of Duccio and Simone Martini (c.1284–1344), but his style owes much to the realism of Giotto (1267–1337). Lorenzetti painted rounded figures and showed a regard for space and depth, although the scale of the background in his work was not always accurate. However, until the early fourteenth century, when architect Filippo Brunelleschi (1377–1446) worked out the mathematical rules of perspective, pictures were composed by eye alone.

The pair of frescoes showing *The Allegory of Good and Bad Government* was commissioned as a piece of civic propaganda for the Sala dei Nove in the Palazzo Pubblico, Siena. Both works were extraordinary at the time for showing a contemporary panorama of a real place with real people.

The *Effects of Good Government* shows Siena as a place of peace and prosperity, with evidence of commerce, active building, agriculture, and industry. Although the frescoes are not dated with certainty, they belong to Lorenzetti's mature work. After 1348 there are no further records of either brother being active and it is thought that they died from the Black Death, which struck Europe that year.

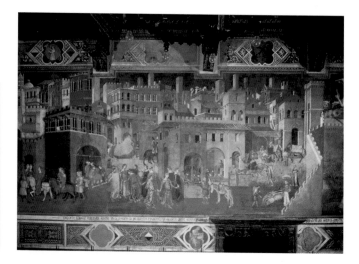

LUCA DELLA ROBBIA (1400–82)

MADONNA AND CHILD (GLAZED TERRACOTTA RELIEF)

The Victoria and Albert Museum, London. Celimage.sa/Lessing Archive

LUCA della Robbia came from a family of artists. Nothing is known of his early career but he was considered by the contemporary art theorist Leon Battista Alberti (1404–72) to be as important an innovator in the new Renaissance style as Donatello and Lorenzo Ghiberti. However, he is now chiefly remembered for the glazed terracotta plaquettes that he introduced as a sculptural medium. The family studio kept the terracotta formula a secret, enabling him to establish a flourishing business.

One of his most famous works, and the first documented of its type, is the *cantoria* (1431–38), or singing gallery, in Florence Cathedral, which shows a cheerful rendition of cherub musicians reflecting antique prototypes. It is paired with a *cantoria* designed by the sculptor Donatello.

The plaquette shown here is one of several half-length, blue-and-white Madonna and Child terracotta reliefs which show that della Robbia's major concern was to represent a three-dimensional shape on a flat plane. The studio was taken over by della Robbia's nephew Andrea (1435–1525), and thereafter by his sons, of whom the most important, artistically, was Giovanni della Robbia (1469–1529).

MASOLINO (DA PANICALE) (C.1383–1447)

SAINT PETER RAISING A CRIPPLE AND THE RESURRECTION OF TABITHA

Brancacci Chapel, Santa Maria del Carmine, Florence. Celimage.sa/Scala Archives

THE first known reference to Masolino occurs in 1423, when he was accepted into the Florentine Guild of Artists, which allowed him to employ assistants in his studio. It is thought that he worked on Lorenzo Ghiberti's first set of Baptistry doors.

Highly regarded in his own time, he has since constantly been compared with Masaccio, who collaborated with him on several works, most importantly the decoration of the Brancacci Chapel in Santa Maria del Carmine, Florence.

In 1426 Masolino went to Hungary with *condottiere* (mercenary) Pippo Spano for two years, leaving Masaccio to continue work on the chapel. Thereafter, Masolino reverted to the International Gothic style, which was still popular in Florence. He traveled to Rome, working in San Clemente, and in 1435 was working in Castiglione d'Olona near Milan.

Naturally a Gothic artist, with a delicate, decorative style, Masolino's work in the Brancacci Chapel does show Masaccio's influence, although their differences in style are marked. This fresco shows two New Testament episodes linked by a pair of foppish, typically sweet-faced young messengers, dressed in flat, rich brocades and showing little urgency for their mission. Significantly, the haloes of Saint Peter and Saint John disobey the rules of perspective.

Early Renaissance

LORENZO GHIBERTI (1378–1455)

JOSEPH SOLD INTO SLAVERY

The Baptistry, Florence. Celimage.sa/Scala Archives

LORENZO Ghiberti, a Florentine goldsmith and sculptor, rose to prominence in 1401 when he won the commission to make one of the two remaining sets of bronze, gilded doors for the Baptistry, beating both sculptor and architect Filippo Brunelleschi and the Sienese sculptor Jacopo della Quercia (1374–1438).

Ghiberti completed the North Doors before working on the East Doors (1425–59), using Donatello's technique of flattened relief. Taking ten Old Testament stories, he created ten panels showing various episodes within masterly compositions of perspective —a contrast to his earlier doors, in which the figures exist as three-dimensional miniatures on a single plane. This panel includes four episodes in the story of Joseph.

The doors were so highly esteemed that they were placed on the east side of the Baptistry, replacing Pisano's earlier creations, where they became a great source of inspiration to other artists. Ghiberti was prominent in the artistic revival of Florence and his large workshop produced several artists of great stature, including Donatello, Masolino, and Paolo Uccello (c.1397–1475). Ghiberti also designed goldsmith's work, reliquaries, and stained-glass windows for Florence Cathedral, and wrote prolifically, leaving the first surviving autobiography of an artist.

FRA ANGELICO (GUIDO DI PIETRO)
(C.1387–1455)

THE ANNUNCIATION

Museo di San Marco, Florence. Celimage.sa/Lessing Archive

FRA Angelico's early career is obscure. He did not take up painting until 1417 and, although his early work was in the International Gothic style, he continued the innovations in perspective introduced by Masaccio.

As a Dominican monk within a teaching order, Fra Angelico's work served a didactic rather than a purely mystical purpose. His style is correspondingly simple, while his contemporaries, such as Masolino, were experimenting with a Neogothic style. Like Fra Filippo Lippi (1406–69), he painted early examples of the *sacra conversazione* (sacred conversation).

In 1438, he and his assistants began painting a series of 50 frescoes to decorate the monks' cells at the monastery of San Marco in Florence. *The Annunciation* is one of these. The frescoes were created as aids to prayer and contemplation; their straightforward composition, limited color, and lack of superfluous detail give them a humble grandeur and serenity. Although Fra Angelico uses the realism and perspectival techniques learned from Masaccio, his haloes and wings are flat, painted in the Gothic style.

Fra Angelico was later commissioned to work at the Vatican, where his frescoes are more ornate, with an emphasis on narrative and detail that was deemed more appropriate for a public palace.

DONATELLO (DONATO DI NICCOLO)
(1386–1466)

DAVID

Museo Nazionale del Bargello, Florence. Celimage.sa/Lessing Archive

A SCULPTOR in marble and bronze, Donatello was the most influential and innovative artist of the early Quattrocento. With his friend Masaccio, and the architects Leon Battista Alberti (1404–72) and Filippo Brunelleschi (1377–1440), he created the monumental realism that was the defining quality of the early Renaissance in Florence.

Trained in Lorenzo Ghiberti's studio, his early commissions included the decorations for the church of Orsanmichele, for which he created vast, freestanding niche statues. Despite the prevailing popularity of the International Gothic style, Donatello created figures of strength and psychological tension, disregarding the surface finish of a sculpture in order to achieve the correct visual effects of light and shade. He was well known for distorting the proportions of his figures. In 1417 Donatello introduced the technique of *rilievo schiacciato* or "flattened relief," as shown in the bas-relief of his Saint George in Orsanmichele. This inspired Ghiberti's East Doors (c.1435) for the Baptistry in Florence.

The elongated, effeminate bronze figure of David shows a Classical concern for anatomy and is thought to be the first nude, freestanding figure made since classical antiquity. In his later years, Donatello experimented with form and content to achieve work of disturbing intensity.

FRA FILIPPO LIPPI (C.1406–69)

THE ANNUNCIATION

San Lorenzo, Florence. Celimage.sa/Lessing Archive

AN orphan, Filippo Lippi grew up in the monastery of the Carmine in Florence, taking holy orders—for which he was unsuited—in 1421. His talent was apparent at an early age and he copied from Masaccio's ground-breaking frescoes in the Brancacci Chapel. Lippi's major achievement is the fresco cycle (1452–66) in the cathedral at Prato. Lippi's patron was Cosimo de' Medici il Vecchio (1389–1464).

Lippi's Barbadori altarpiece (1437) in Santo Spirito, Florence, is one of the first datable examples of the *sacra conversazione*, in which the Virgin, Child, and saints inhabit the same space—a format that superseded the Virgin and Child enthroned, with saints arranged in panels on either side.

Lippi's work shows the profound influence of both Masaccio and Donatello, but he replaces the chiaroscuro, solidity, and prescribed space of Masaccio with a sweeter, linear style reminiscent of the Gothic style. The altarpiece also shows the influence of Flemish art, most noticeable in the translucent vase in the foreground.

ANDREA MANTEGNA (1431–1506)

CHRIST IN THE GARDEN OF OLIVES

Musée des Beaux-Arts, Tours. Celimage.sa/Lessing Archive

PUPIL and adopted son of Francesco Squarcione (1397–c.1468), Mantegna grew up in Padua, and was surrounded by humanist ideas, Classical nude studies and the sculptures of Donatello, all of which influenced his style. His paintings were marked by a passion for Classical architecture and a mastery of perspective and foreshortening—qualities evident by 1448 when he began a series of frescoes for the Ovetari Chapel in Eremetani Church, Padua, which was destroyed in 1944.

In 1460 Mantegna became court painter to Ludovico Gonzaga at Mantua—a town that rivaled the artistic centers of Rome and Florence. He decorated the Ducal Palace with frescoes glorifying the Gonzaga family. Most notably, he introduced the Classical feature of painting illusory architecture that seems to extend into a real perspective. The same technique was also used by Raphael (1483–1520) and Correggio (c.1490–1534), but not fully exploited until the Baroque period in the seventeenth century.

Christ In The Garden Of Olives, based on a sketch by Jacopo Bellini (c.1400–70), is an excellent example of the sharp, analytical style of Mantegna's work. Other pieces, such as the *Crucifixion* (c.1459), are notable for their innovative compositions. Mantegna's experiments with viewpoints and the sculpted and tinted stone or bronze quality of his forms also illustrate the influence of Donatello.

Early Renaissance

PIERO DELLA FRANCESCA (C.1416–92)

FEDERIGO DA MONTEFELTRO, DUKE OF URBINO

Uffizi Gallery, Florence. Celimage.sa/Lessing Archive

PIERO della Francesca's work is remarkable for its synthesis of mid-fifteenth-century Italian painting, with its deep interest in perspective and space, and Flemish painting, with all its study of light, bright colors and natural phenomena and detail. His work is dominated by a serene grandeur, and has very little sense of movement. Instead, it is based on the strict mathematical principles of geometry and perspective.

Moving from his home town of Borgo San Sepolcro to Florence, Piero was influenced by the work of Fra Angelico and Paolo Uccello, from whom he derived his solid figures, love of color, and fascination with perspective and space. He absorbed the influences of Flemish art, which was beginning to infiltrate Florentine culture in the 1430s. After 1442 he worked in Ferrara, Rimini, Arezzo, Rome, and Urbino. The frescoes at Arezzo (1452–c.1459), which depict *The Story of the True Cross*, are among his most important works. The *Brera Madonna* (c.1475), one of his last works, is an early *sacra conversazione* piece, with a use of perspective that seems to expand into the church.

The Flemish influences on Piero's work can be seen in this portrait of his patron, the Duke of Urbino, in the play of light, the details of hair and skin, the background landscape, and the oil medium.

PAOLO UCCELLO (C.1396–1475)

THE HUNT IN THE FOREST

Ashmolean Museum, Oxford. Celimage.sa/Lessing Archive

UCCELLO was apprenticed to Lorenzo Ghiberti between 1407 and 1415, although he never worked as a sculptor. In 1425 he went to Venice to work as a mosaicist and returned to Florence by 1432, where he produced two frescoes depicting scenes from the Old Testament in the Green Cloister in Santa Maria Novella. These were organized across a single plane in which linear perspective was not used. His first dated work of 1436, a large fresco of the English mercenary Sir John Hawkwood, reveals his newfound fascination with perspective.

Uccello's work combines both the decorative, elaborate spirit of the International Gothic style, which he would have learned in Ghiberti's studio, with the new laws of early Renaissance perspective. He is often considered to have been somewhat fanatical about the treatment of perspective in painting, although he did not always get it right. *The Deluge* (1445), also in the Green Cloister, shows the impact of the new ideas on perspective at their most powerful.

This painting, generally considered a late work and painted in oil on panel, combines Gothic and early Renaissance styles with a fairy-tale charm. Although in some ways the regularity of the design creates an almost medieval effect, the movement of the dogs and horses balances the composition with a darting energy.

ANTONIO DEL POLLAIUOLO (C.1432-98)

HERCULES AND THE GIANT ANTAIOS

Uffizi Gallery, Florence. Celimage.sa/Lessing Archive

THE Pollaiuolo brothers were goldsmiths, engravers, sculptors, painters, and designers of embroideries, and owned one of the most successful workshops in Florence during the second half of the fifteenth century. There are few known works by Piero—it appears that Antonio was largely responsible for most of the work of quality that emerged from their workshop.

The brothers' work is characterized by a fascination with the human body in motion. Their capacity to model realistic three-dimensional figures was based on a thorough understanding of human anatomy. The influences of Donatello, a key figure in Renaissance sculpture, and Andrea del Castagno (c.1421–57), known for his powerful portrayal of figures, are paramount in their work—Piero is thought to have been a pupil of del Castagno.

Hercules and the Giant Antaios is a powerful display of heroic energy, achieved through the characters' pose, or rhythmic accent. They dominate the scene, two men of equal weight wrestling to prevail. Hercules is depicted as being as large as the giant, and there is an animal quality to the image.

ANTONELLO DA MESSINA (C.1430–79)

PORTRAIT OF A MAN

Thyssen-Bornemisza Collection, Madrid. Celimage.sa/Lessing Archive

ANTONELLO da Messina, a Sicilian, was the only major fifteenth-century painter born south of Rome. He trained in Naples, where he was influenced by Flemish painters, particularly Jan van Eyck. His first known work is a portrait of Salvator Muni (1465). In 1475–76 he visited Venice, and had a profound effect on the artistic community. His Flemish realism and attention to detail, combined with the grandeur of Italian art, was revolutionary. He popularized the use of oils—a technique widespread in northern Europe but little used in Italy.

Da Messina's most influential work in Venice was the San Cassiano altarpiece, of which two fragments remain. In the *sacra conversazione,* the setting of the painting extends by *trompe-l'oeil* into the chapel itself—the Madonna, Child, and saints appear to inhabit the same space as the viewer.

Portrait of a Man reveals da Messina's Flemish influences—in the three-quarter, rather than the side, view, the lively glance, and the precise detail. The dark background and the light used to accentuate the clearly modeled features, were northern techniques for focusing attention on the face.

Early Renaissance

ANDREA DELLA ROBBIA (1435–1525)

MADONNA OF THE GOLDFINCH

LaVerna, Sanctuary. Celimage.sa/Scala Archives

ANDREA della Robbia was Luca della Robbia's nephew, and the most important of his successors. Luca was the most successful artist of the family, and he trained his nephew in both marble and ceramics. We can see strong parallels between the work of the two artists, specifically with reference to their Madonna and Child terracotta plaquettes. Both display an allegiance to Renaissance and Neo-Classical styles of work. Luca was in fact to become a leading exponent of Renaissance art.

Luca's influence can be seen in Andrea's *Madonna of the Goldfinch*, in the way that both artists were preoccupied with the presentation of a three-dimensional shape on a flat plane. Andrea also specialized in the production of narrative sculpture. His most famous work is *The Foundling Children* (1463–66), which were ten round sculptures of infants swaddled in cloth.

In this terracotta work, the two white-cream figures are framed by a bright blue sky. The detail of their faces and expressions is extremely realistic, and the plain color of their faces symbolizes their purity. The frame of green foliage contributes to the work's decorative nature.

During the late fifteenth century Andrea continued his uncle's business in glazed terracotta sculpture, and they shared the same furnace until Luca's death in 1482. By 1455, Andrea was working autonomously.

CARLO CRIVELLI (C.1435–95)

CORONATION OF THE VIRGIN, WITH SAINTS JOHN BAPTIST, MARY MAGDALEN (LEFT), FRANCIS OF ASSISI, AND SAINT AUGUSTINE (RIGHT)

Pinacoteca di Brera, Milan. Celimage.sa/Lessing Archive

CARLO Crivelli was a Venetian and a contemporary of the Bellini brothers and Andrea Mantegna. In 1457 he was expelled from Venice for committing adultery, first working in Dalmatia (now Croatia) and then moving to the Italian Marches: he never returned to Venice after this, but always persisted in signing himself as a Venetian.

As a result, Crivelli worked in an artistic vacuum, away from the great Renaissance centers of Florence, Venice, and Rome. Before his expulsion he may have worked in the Vivarini workshop in Venice. He may have had some experience in Padua, where it is possible that he absorbed influences from Mantegna—his work has the same attention to detail and interest in classical archeology.

Crivelli's paintings have an exacting quality, evident in the clarity of the drawing, the contours of the figures and objects, and his use of bright colors. *The Coronation of the Virgin* displays a complicated iconography, in which the fruits and garlands that adorn his work play a part.

Early Renaissance

41

GIOVANNI BELLINI (C.1430–1516)

MADONNA OF THE SMALL TREES

Accademia Gallery, Venice. Celimage.sa/Scala Archives

GIOVANNI Bellini was first active in about 1445. Although he was trained by his father Jacopo, his most important influence was Andrea Mantegna. Bellini was known for the soft quality of his work and was an excellent portraitist. He was the civic painter of Venice, and Titian (c.1485–1576) and Giorgione (c.1477–1510) trained in his studio. He, his father, and his elder brother, Gentile (c.1429–1507), are credited with transforming the art of Venice to rival that of Florence and Rome.

Always open to new ideas, Bellini was influenced by Antonello da Messina to become one of the earliest masters of the oil technique. Oils allowed the linearity of his early work to give way to light and color as the two most important means of expression. He was also one of the first artists to create architectural settings for his *sacra conversazione* pieces, so that they appeared to extend into the space of the real architecture.

In his portraiture, Bellini often used the Flemish three-quarter profile against a landscape. He was primarily a religious painter, particularly of Madonnas, and was known for the serenity and sympathy of his figures and for the inventiveness of his designs. *Madonna of the Small Trees* shows his precision in rendering light and shade, and his faultless sense of perspective.

ANDREA DEL VERROCCHIO
(ANDREA DI CIONI) (1435–88)

MONUMENT TO BARTOLOMMEO COLLEONI

Campo dei Santi Giovanni e Paolo, Venice. Celimage.sa/Lessing Archive

ANDREA del Verrocchio became the leading sculptor in Florence after Donatello's death. He was trained as a goldsmith, painter, and sculptor, and may have been taught by Donatello, but his style refers more to the Romantic sensitivity of the latter half of the fifteenth century.

Verrocchio's two-statue group of *Christ and Saint Thomas* (1467–83) was one of the largest to have been commissioned at that time. It was designed to fit into a niche in Orsanmichele, Florence, which had originally been intended for one statue, revealing the artist's versatility. It also shows the lightness, elegance of pose, and high craftsmanship for which he was renowned. Most of the artists who were active around 1490 studied at Verrocchio's workshop. He was Leonardo da Vinci's (1452–1519) master and is said to have been so overwhelmed by the angel in Leonardo's *Baptism of Christ* that he decided never to paint again. Certainly, after this time, he seems to have concentrated solely on producing his sculpture.

His major sculptural works are *David* (1473–75) and this, his last commission, the superb equestrian statue of the Venetian warlord Bartolommeo Colleoni, which is still on display in Venice.

SANDRO BOTTICELLI (ALESSANDRO DI MARIANO FILIPEPI) (C.1445–1510)

THE BIRTH OF VENUS

Uffizi Gallery, Florence. Celimage.sa/Lessing Archive

SANDRO Botticelli was one of the greatest and most popular Italian masters of the late fifteenth century. His graceful, rounded style and the projection of a sense of spirituality in his work were the result of an apprenticeship with Filippo Lippi. He later worked with the Pollaiuolo brothers, absorbing their naturalism as well as their techniques of foreshortening and perspective.

Botticelli reacted against the realism of Masaccio by reviving elements of Gothic art—a delicacy of sentiment, expressed in an ornamental style—that he imbued with freshness and beauty. He worked in tempera, usually on panel, and painted portraits as well as religious, political, and mythological works full of allegory as well as symbolism.

In 1481 he was called to Rome to paint part of the Sistine Chapel. Returning to Florence in 1484, his style became harsher and he withdrew from public life to illustrate Dante Alighieri's *Inferno*, written in c.1307. During his lifetime, Botticelli's style was viewed as archaic, especially when compared with Renaissance artists such as Leonardo da Vinci (1425–1519), Raphael (1483–1520), and Michelangelo (1475–1564), and he died in obscurity.

The Medici family, the great Renaissance patrons of Florentine art, commissioned *The Birth of Venus*, showing the Roman goddess of love and beauty rising from the sea on a sculpted seashell.

FILIPPINO LIPPI (C.1457–1504)

PORTRAIT OF AN OLD MAN

Uffizi Gallery, Florence. Celimage.sa/Lessing Archive

FILIPPINO Lippi was the son and pupil of Fra Filippo Lippi and, after his father's death in 1469, the pupil of Botticelli. His work is often overshadowed by that of his two masters. Filippino's first major commission came in 1484 when he was asked to complete Masaccio's frescoes in the Brancacci Chapel of Santa Maria del Carmine in Florence, which he did with sensitivity. From these works, Lippi first made his name as an artist.

His most important frescoes are those of the *Life of Saint Thomas Aquinas* (1488–93) in the Caffa Chapel in Santa Maria sopra Minerva, Rome, and the *Lives of Saint Philip and Saint John* (1487–1502) in the Strozzi Chapel in Santa Maria Novella, Florence. In these he created picturesque yet dramatic effects which, combined with a graceful quality, identify him as one of the most inventive of Italy's late-fifteenth-century artists.

This painting illustrates his robust style. He was a master of expression—note the wrinkles on the old man's face and the resigned posture of his slightly bowed head and crossed arms, all lit from a single source to the left.

GENTILE BELLINI (C.1429–1507)

THE MIRACLE OF THE TRUE CROSS
NEAR SAN LORENZO BRIDGE

Accademia Gallery, Venice. Celimage.sa/Lessing Archive

GENTILE Bellini, the elder son of Jacopo Bellini (c.1400–70), was trained by his father in Venice. His first known work, a portrait of Lorenzo Giustiniani, the first patriarch of the city, dates from 1465. A year later he worked with his father, as well as Bartolommeo Vivarini (1432–99) and Francesco Squarcione, the adopted father of Andrea Mantegna, on a series of frescoes for the Scuola di San Marco in Venice. Soon afterwards he was appointed official portraitist in Venice and between 1479–81 his skills took him to Constantinople as portraitist to Sultan Mehmet II, where he absorbed the influences of Eastern, Byzantine-influenced art.

In 1474 Gentile began a series of history paintings in the Council Chamber in the Doge's palace, which were destroyed by fire in 1577. He also produced portrait groups that included views of Venice, and a number of large, propaganda-based civic canvases depicting religious incidents from Venice's history. *The Miracle of the True Cross near San Lorenzo Bridge* is one such work. Painted in oil, it is one of three works for the *Cycle of the True Cross* painted for the Scuola di San Giovanni and is typical for its anecdotal qualities and attention to detail. The painting is suffused with soft light which dwells on the crowd and highlights the stunning Venetian architecture in detail.

DOMENICO GHIRLANDAIO (1449–94)

OLD MAN AND HIS GRANDSON

Louvre, Paris. Celimage.sa/Lessing Archive

BORN in Florence, Domenico Ghirlandaio originally trained as a goldsmith; this explains, in part, his highly decorative style and extensive use of gold embellishments. He worked predominantly in the field of fresco painting, and once said that he would like to decorate every wall of every building. He became a popular and prolific fresco artist in Florence, receiving many prestigious commissions. He passed on his great skill to his most famous apprentice, Michelangelo (1475–1564).

Many of Ghirlandaio's frescoes, although intended to depict religious narratives, also contain portraits of key figures and patrons of Florence society. A similar personalization is apparent in his anachronistic settings: fashionable, wealthy Florence is often used as the backdrop for his biblical scenes. The inclusion of contemporary details in frescoes of this era was criticized by some as obtrusive and unrealistic; however, this technique helped to give the works more immediacy, bringing the biblical stories into the realm of the artist and viewer of the time.

A key element of Ghirlandaio's success was the realistic detail he applied to his representations of people, a realism that is evident in *Old Man and His Grandson*, in which the master has taken the "warts and all" approach.

Early Renaissance

JEAN, PAUL, AND HERMAN LIMBOURG

"JANUARY" FROM
LES TRÈS RICHES HEURES DU DUC DU BERRY

Musée Condé, Chantilly. Celimage.sa/Lessing Archive

THE artistic partnership of the three Limbourg brothers created this celebrated illuminated prayer book, one of several known as "books of hours," the "hours" were in the form of prayers to be recited at set times throughout the day. The exquisite depictions of courtly love and chivalric imagery contain powerful and enduring iconography.

The Limbourg brothers, who were born in Flanders but worked in France, gained international acceptance for their highly desirable Flemish style, which was well expressed in manuscript form. The style was renowned for its rich, bright colors and reproductions of landscape directly from nature, a pioneering approach that was to have a profound effect on French art and led to the evolution of realism later in the fifteenth century.

Les Très Riches Heures was commissioned by the Duke of Berry—he was one of the era's most important art collectors and brother of the powerful Duke of Burgundy (Philip the Good, 1419–67). The duke was renowned for his raids on Europe and the East for art treasures. The month of "January," with its carnival of color and highly decorative detail, shows the duke probably returning from a raid to a sumptuous court banquet.

GENTILE DA FABRIANO (C.1370–1427)

THE PRESENTATION OF THE CHILD
IN THE TEMPLE

Louvre, Paris. Celimage.sa/Lessing Archive

GENTILE da Fabriano's work is a stunning example of the blending of International Gothic style with the early Renaissance works of fifteenth-century Florence. During this period the Lombardy and Venetian regions of Italy were artistically closer to the development in oils associated with the Flanders workshops than to nearby Florence.

Da Fabriano's fascination with detail and vignettes of jewelry, birds, and dogs are similar to Giotto's earlier creations. He created a vibrant effect, seen in this intricately worked piece and his other celebrated masterpiece, *Adoration of the Magi* (1423).

The effects of humanist philosophy on the fourteenth century broke art's bondage to theology, allowing some acknowledgement of the "real," secular world. The International Gothic movement allowed intuition to take the lead. The representational lyricism of *The Presentation of the Child in the Temple* reflects this move, although medieval problems concerning space and depth are still an issue. Here, notions of perspective are accomplished through strong bands of horizontal line, the use of a central light source in the main tableau, and the angular forms of the buildings.

International Gothic

ROBERT CAMPIN (C.1375–1444)

SAINT JOHN BAPTIST AND THE FRANCISCAN THEOLOGIAN HEINRICH VON WERL (LEFT) AND SAINT BARBARA (RIGHT)

Prado, Madrid. Celimage.sa/Lessing Archive

KNOWN as the Master of Flémalle, Campin, alongside Jan van Eyck (1390–1441), was one of the most influential masters of the early Flemish school. Working at Tournai in Flanders, he was one of the first artists to experiment with the reintroduction of oil-based colors, to achieve the brilliance of color typical with this period.

Campin used the new technique to convey strong, rounded characters by modeling light and shade in compositions of complex perspectives. A pioneer of new facial types and characteristics, Campin was the first artist to try to capture and portray in his painting the sitter's personality. He was also bold in experimenting with traditional religious imagery, creating a cosy Flanders home setting for his *Merode Annunciation* triptych (1428), instead of the traditional gold backdrop.

The Werl altarpiece was a triptych, the central panel of which has been lost. The left wing depicts the donor, Heinrich von Werl, a theologian from Cologne. He is flanked by Saint John Baptist.

JAN VAN EYCK (C.1390–1441)

THE ARNOLFINI MARRIAGE

The National Gallery, London. Celimage.sa/Lessing Archive

THE early Flemish school's greatest artist, Jan van Eyck, along with his contemporary, Rogier van der Weyden (1399–1464), was responsible for the spread of the International Gothic style. He worked for the Duke of Burgundy, acted as court envoy to Spain and Portugal and as diplomat and city official in Bruges from 1430. Some believe he invented oil painting because of his advanced use of the medium. In fact, this technique had been known since antiquity, but van Eyck used it as never before to portray sensational lighting effects of great clarity and realism.

His skilful development of oil's translucent properties is explored in a variety of textures in this landmark double portrait, one of the greatest pictures of the second millennium. It was probably a bourgeois commission to commemorate the couple's betrothal; as such, it is one of the very first genre paintings, in a style that depicts the lives of ordinary people rather than concentrating solely on the portrayal of religious subjects.

Although ignorant of one-point perspective, van Eyck achieves visual balance through a subtly lit interior and compositional symmetry, with the medial line of the perfectly centralized mirror falling between the couple.

ANTONIO PISANELLO (C.1395–1455)

LIONEL D'ESTE

Accademia Carrara Gallery, Bergamo. Celimage.sa/Lessing Archive

THE successor to Gentile da Fabriano, Pisanello worked in Verona. Like his master, he was fascinated with the bejeweled tapestry effects that could be created using the new oil medium that had been pioneered by the Flanders workshops. The medium suited the climate of Italy much better than the cold, damp Low Countries of northern Europe. Pisanello painted frescoes at Verona in Italy, where two survive, and also in Venice and Rome, though these have since been destroyed.

Pisanello's work is characterized by naturalism and a detailed observation of reality. Despite the obvious influence of the International Gothic style, he shared the Florentine preoccupation with structure, foreshortening, and one-point perspective in his draftsmanship.

The most renowned court painter and medallist of his time, Pisanello was a draftsman of genius: his drawings became models for the later Renaissance artists. This portrait of Lionel d'Este, a member of one of Verona's chief families and a patron of the arts, reveals his wonderful manipulation of oil and his subtle introduction of light.

ROGIER VAN DER WEYDEN (1399–1464)

SAINT CATHERINE

Kunsthistorisches Museum, Gemaeldegalerie, Vienna. Celimage.sa/Lessing Archive

AFTER Jan van Eyck, Rogier van der Weyden was the most influential Flemish artist of the fifteenth century. He traveled widely throughout Europe, encouraging the adoption of revolutionary new oil techniques to achieve effects of realism and natural light. No signed paintings have survived and little is known about van der Weyden's life except that he was probably apprenticed to Roger Campin, the Master of Flémalle.

Van der Weyden lived in Brussels and became the city's official painter in 1436. He traveled to Italy in 1450, influencing painting there and absorbing the Italian trend for a warm, bright palette. Like the Limbourg brothers before him, he was commissioned by the Duke of Burgundy to paint court portraits, spreading his artistic authority into France.

His lighting had a profound impact on religious art, bathing the subject's symbolic detail in an other-worldly atmosphere. Warmer in palette than van Eyck, he was less concerned with the realistic representation of space. His work pioneered the projection of mood and emotion in painting, seen here in *Saint Catherine*.

BENOZZO GOZZOLI (C.1421–97)

THE JOURNEY OF THE MAGI (DETAIL)

Palazzo Medici-Riccardi, Florence. Celimage.sa/Scala Archives

THE Florentine painter Gozzoli took over the poetic mantle of Gentile da Fabriano in producing richly tapestried landscapes of immense beauty and color. In his youth he was an assistant to Lorenzo Ghiberti (1378–1455), working on the Baptistry doors in Florence. He also assisted Fra Angelico (c.1387–1455) with frescoes in the Vatican, but later gained a reputation as a painter in his own right.

The International Gothic style synthesized the decorative elements of the Flemish school with the realism of Italian art, and in Gozzoli's painting we can see a renewed sensitivity to landscape settings, a progression in the use of new facial types, and further attempts at the portrayal of psychological characteristics in the individuals depicted in the paintings.

In *The Journey of the Magi*, Gozzoli shows an awareness of depth and spatial values. Bands of color are broken up by the structural element of the zigzagging road that runs up the center of the picture line to create a sensation of distance and horizon, as well as movement. Gozzoli's most famous fresco, it was painted in the small chapel of the Palazzo Medici-Riccardi in Florence, during the hot summer of 1459, which explains the brilliance of the gold and azure lighting effects.

DIERIC BOUTS (C.1415–75)

VIRGIN AND CHILD

Fine Arts Royal Museum, Antwerp. Celimage.sa/Scala Archives

BELIEVED to be a pupil of Rogier van der Weyden, Bouts shared his master's love of rich color and realism, exploring their effects on spatial relationships, perspective, and composition. A native of Haarlem, he moved to Louvain in the more prosperous south of the Low Countries, which brought him closer to Brussels and the great studios of van Eyck and van der Weyden. Under their influence, his distinctive style gained maturity and control, enabling him to express a deep spiritual beauty through a portrayal of detached stillness similar to van Eyck's. He became Louvain's civic painter in 1468, and one of his commissions was the *Last Supper* triptych, which he painted in the last years of his life.

Bouts worked on highly polished wood panels, using oils mixed with color pigments to achieve a transparent finish and brilliant color. The fine details seen in his work, which were executed with minute brushstrokes, reveal his mastery of his medium, as shown in this tender work.

The Virgin's face is rendered with an acute level of psychological understanding, and expresses the tenderness she feels for Christ, just as any mother would feel for her son. Bouts achieves a sense of tranquillity in the work by surrounding the mother and baby with a shimmering gold light.

HANS MEMLING (C.1433–94)

THE MYSTIC MARRIAGE OF SAINT CATHERINE

Memling Museum, Bruges. Celimage.sa/Scala Archives

BORN near Frankfurt, Hans Memling was a pupil of the highly influential Flemish master Rogier van der Weyden, and worked mainly in Bruges, Flanders, in an atmosphere that became increasingly conservative as the century progressed. His sensitive portrait work is highly accomplished. His paintings influenced artists beyond Flanders, although they are overshadowed by the work of his master, van der Weyden. However, Memling's quiet, contemplative style was highly successful in his day.

This composition, part of a triptych, was painted for the Hôpital de St Jean in Bruges. The two other side panels depict complex images: *Beheading the Baptist* and *The Vision of Saint John the Evangelist on Patmos*.

Using a technique developed by van der Weyden, Memling paints the folded flowing drapery of the two seated female saints, Catherine and Barbara, in a way that injects energy into an otherwise static, stolidly composed scene. Memling developed this technique in a later work, *The Shrine of Saint Ursula* (1489), which had a narrative style that impacted on early Renaissance Italian artists such as Vittore Carpaccio (c.1455–1525).

HIERONYMUS BOSCH (C.1450–1516)

THE GARDEN OF EARTHLY DELIGHTS

Prado Museum, Madrid. Celimage.sa/Lessing Archive

ONE of the last of the great medieval Flemish painters, Bosch explored a highly imaginative world of religious symbolism and allegory, from horrific images of hell through to visions of heavenly delight.

Weird, colorful, and playful, he ignored the influences of the early Italian Renaissance, which were beginning to spread across the cultural divides of Europe. Bosch's sense of color and form seems strikingly modern, and analogies have been drawn between his work and that of the twentieth century's Expressionist and Surrealist movements. Although he knew the pioneering realism of the works of Flemish painters such as Jan van Eyck and Robert Campin, he developed his own fantastical style, with depictions of distorted creatures reminiscent of Classical "grotesque" imagery—chaotic mural decorations of flora and fauna. He was very popular in his lifetime and his works were often forged.

In this stunning triptych, each panel is endowed with its own meaning. The landscape is minutely detailed, brightly colored, and freakish, complemented by bizarre imaginary creatures and figures. A fourth painting, *The Third Day of Creation*, is revealed when the triptych is closed.

MATTHIAS GRÜNEWALD (C.1475–1528)

THE CRUCIFIXION

Musée d'Unterlinden, Colmar. Celimage.sa/Lessing Archive

THE graphic horror and emotional intensity of the International Gothic artists is felt particularly in the work of German artist Matthias Grünewald. A contemporary of Albrecht Dürer (1471–1528), his art verges on the macabre, with dark, somber imagery and themes.

He is renowned for his series of ten paintings for the cathedral altar in Isenheim, Alsace. They were intended to be seen in three groups, which changed as the altar panels were alternately opened and closed.

The undercurrent of violence in this scene is acute, as the mutilated body of Christ expires in agony on the oversized cross, which bends with the weight of his slumped torso. The hands are distorted in the final moment of anguish. The faithful mourners grouped below the cross are oddly set against the exaggerated form of Christ. All this is placed in the dark setting of a wasteland, quite unlike the glowing tapestry of color used by early exponents of the International Gothic style such as Gentile da Fabriano. Yet the very freedom of expression inherent in the ideals of the International Gothic movement allowed the creative impetus necessary for the portrayal of such naked, anguished emotion.

PERUGINO (PIETRO VANNUCCI) (C.1445–1523)

MADONNA DEL SACCO

Galleria Palatina, Florence. Celimage.sa/Scala Archives

THE Umbrian master Perugino was born in Città della Pieve. During the late 1460s he moved to Florence to study with Andrea del Verrochio, the master who also taught Leonardo da Vinci. Perugino's work became highly prized toward the end of the fifteenth century, but a decade later was criticized for being repetitious and formulaic. He often reused cartoons, probably due to the large volume of work undertaken by his studios in Perugia and Florence.

From 1481, with Botticelli and Ghirlandaio, Perugino decorated the walls of the Sistine Chapel with fresco paintings depicting scenes from the Old and New Testaments as well as portraits of several popes. Today he is chiefly remembered as Raphael's master. Both artists painted luxuriously colored, sculptural robes which emphasized the Classical quality of their gracefully posed figures.

The *Madonna del Sacco* shows two key features of Perugino's work: his figure painting, in the conventional style of Florentine artists of the time; and his use of Umbrian landscapes in earthy colors to form a strong contrast with the brightness of the robes.

LEONARDO DA VINCI (1452–1519)

MONA LISA

Louvre, Paris. Celimage.sa/Lessing Archive

LEONARDO was a formidable genius who, with Michelangelo and Raphael, shaped and accelerated the great changes that took place in the period known as the High Renaissance. Born in 1452 in Tuscany, Leonardo was apprenticed to the sculptor Andrea del Verrocchio. From 1482 he worked at the court of Milan—not solely as an artist, for he possessed great skills and knowledge in many areas: he was a talented scientific investigator, engineer, architect, and designer. Few of his completed paintings survive, but those that remain show his remarkable talent. Leonardo pioneered many new artistic techniques that were later copied and developed by his contemporaries. One such technique was *sfumato*, meaning to give the appearance of imperceptible changes in gradation of light, so that harsh outlines took on a softened appearance.

This technique was employed in the *Mona Lisa*, arguably the most famous painting in the history of Western art, which has become almost an icon of art itself. A serenely smiling woman, whose identity still remains unknown, appears in front of a mist-strewn rocky landscape, which further increases the painting's enigmatic qualities.

MICHELANGELO BUONARROTI (1475–1564)

DAVID

Accademia Gallery, Florence. Celimage.sa/Scala Archives

MICHELANGELO was born in Caprese and was apprenticed to the Florentine master Domenico Ghirlandaio. His talents were soon recognized by Lorenzo de' Medici, who took the young artist into his home. While with the Medici family, Michelangelo was able to study their impressive collection of classical antiquities. Such studies clearly had a great impact on his work from the beginning, as seen in his very early pieces such as *The Madonna of the Steps* (1491–92).

Michelangelo's greatest interest lay in sculpture, but it was the series of fresco paintings he carried out on the ceiling of the Sistine Chapel (1508–12), regarded as one of the crowning achievements of the High Renaissance, that ultimately consolidated his fame, begun with the completion of his sculptural works *Pietà* (1498–99) and *David*. Michelangelo was also a creative architect and talented poet.

Throughout his career Michelangelo sculpted and painted images of young male nudes, beautifully formed and gracefully poised. In *David*, Michelangelo's early study of human anatomy is evident in the superbly realistic form of the young man who stands with sling held lightly, waiting for his enemy to come into range.

SODOMA (BAZZI), GIOVANNI ANTONIO
(1477–1549)

VENUS TERRESTRE WITH EROS AND VENUS CELESTE WITH ANTEROS AND TWO CUPIDS

Louvre, Paris. Celimage.sa/Lessing Archive

GIOVANNI Bazzi, known as Il Sodoma, was born in Lombardy. He was the son of a shoemaker and it was alleged by writers of the time that he earned his nickname because of his homosexuality; if this is true, then it was a name that he was pleased with, as he used it as his signature consistently throughout his life.

In 1490, at the age of 13, Sodoma was apprenticed to Giovanni Spanzotti in Vercelli, where he stayed until 1498 when he moved to Milan. Leonardo da Vinci was working in Milan during the same period and his effect on Sodoma is apparent in the latter's works thereafter, particularly the *sfumato* effect seen in many of his paintings. From 1500 Sodoma was working in Siena, where the majority of his works were undertaken, and indeed he dominated the Sienese art scene for several years, although he also worked in Rome. In 1508 Sodoma was among the elite group of artists who were commissioned by the Pope to decorate the papal rooms at the Vatican.

Venus terrestre with Eros and Venus celeste with Anteros and two cupids shows Sodoma's intimate treatment of the human form. This gentle allegorical scene shows a tender encounter between the participants, set against a wonderfully embellished frame of figures and natural motifs.

GIORGIONE (C.1477–1510)

THE TEMPEST

Accademia Gallery, Florence. Celimage.sa/Scala Archives

THE life of Giorgione (Giorgio Barbarelli) is largely a mystery. It is known that he was apprenticed to Giovanni Bellini and that he later collaborated with several other major artists. The veracity of some of his works has been questioned because of these collaborations; also, his untimely death in 1510 meant that unfinished paintings were completed by other artists. Despite his short career and the small number of completed works, Giorgione's impact on art has been both great and lasting. In particular, his influence on Venetian artists was immense—his superb use of color had a profound effect on his student Titian's (c.1488–1576) artistic development. The predominance of landscape and its naturalistic portrayal crop up in the work of many later artists.

The Tempest is perhaps Giorgione's most famous painting. The subject matter, like his life, is perplexing. The identity of the naked woman, and the significance of the male figure watching her, are unclear; any interpretation of the piece remains subjective. Such strange and enigmatic themes were unusual in Renaissance art: more commonly, well-known religious or mythical subjects were commissioned and portrayed.

RAPHAEL (1483–1520)

THE SCHOOL OF ATHENS

Stanze della Segnatura, Vatican City, Rome. Celimage.sa/Lessing Archive

BORN in Urbino, Raphael was the son of a painter. He showed artistic talent from a young age, and at 17 was studying with the master Perugino. Raphael was approaching adulthood while the influence on the art world of Michelangelo and Leonardo became apparent. For several years he lived in Florence, where they were working; Leonardo's influential *sfumato* style can be seen in much of Raphael's work during this period. He had an innate ability to absorb the innovations of other artists; he did not mimic their style but understood and developed their techniques in such a way as to express his own vision.

In 1508 Raphael was summoned to Rome by the Pope, who commissioned him to decorate the private papal rooms of the Sistine Chapel; concurrently, Michelangelo was working on the ceiling of the chapel. There was some considerable professional rivalry between the two artists. *The School of Athens* was painted in the Stanza della Segnatura at the Vatican. Framed within a superb architectural setting, the philosophers of the ancient world converse; our eye is drawn to the two central figures of Aristotle and Plato. In this painting, Raphael's perfect rendering of the harmonious balance attempted in earlier Classical art holds the key to his importance during and after the High Renaissance.

FRA BARTOLOMMEO DELLA PORTA
(C.1472–1517)

NOLI ME TANGERE

Louvre, Paris. Celimage.sa/Lessing Archive

FRA Bartolommeo was apprenticed to Cosimo Rosselli (1439–1507) in 1484. He was deeply affected by the puritanical teachings of the controversial Florentine monk Savonarola, after whose death, in 1498, he took holy orders at San Marco monastery in Florence. He then set about destroying all his works containing nudes, considering them sinful, and did not resume painting until 1504, when he became head of the monastery workshop.

His intention in painting was to instill religious devotion in his audience. His works are characterized by a religious intimacy—particularly his Madonnas. He visited Venice in 1508 and Rome in 1514, both visits helping him to develop the balance and simplicity of his paintings. Fra Bartolommeo was one of the first artists to use dress to emphasize the difference between the human and the divine in painting—his religious figures do not wear contemporary clothes.

Noli me Tangere shows the expressive gestures, rapt expressions, and simplicity of setting that are typical of his work.

High Renaissance

LORENZO LOTTO (1480–1557)

PORTRAIT OF A HUSBAND AND WIFE

Hermitage, St Petersburg. Celimage.sa/Lessing Archive

LOTTO was born in Venice, where he trained as an artist. However, he was distanced from other Italian artists by his style of painting, which was unfashionable in an age dominated by the two great Venetian painters Titian (c.1488–1576) and Tintoretto (1518–94). Lotto was a unique artist, with a vision that enabled him to create remarkable paintings which have a contemporary resonance. His realistic and empathetic works, filled with distinctive sharp lines and vivid colors, lean toward Flemish art rather than Venetian. Consequently, during his lifetime Lotto did not achieve the level of success that his accomplished and emotive paintings deserved; he died penniless, having joined a religious order in 1554. For centuries Lotto was largely ignored by art critics, and it was only in the twentieth century that his reputation was restored.

Lotto's most successful paintings were portraits. The *Portrait of a Husband and Wife* is a fine example of his vivid style, not least for its depiction of symbolic objects such as the squirrel and the sheet of paper with the inscription that reads "Man not animal." Lotto's penchant for including symbolic references in his paintings has led some to describe him as a forerunner to the Surrealists.

JACOPO TINTORETTO (1519–94)

THE LAST SUPPER

Scuola Grande di S. Rocco, Venice. Celimage.sa/Scala Archives

BORN in Venice, Jacopo Tintoretto seldom left the place of his birth. He was given the nickname Il Tintoretto, meaning "little dyer," because his father was a cloth dyer. Although he was the most prolific of all the Venetian artists, he did not gain the level of prestige usually attributed to masters—possibly due to his artisan background. To complete the vast number of commissions he accepted, Tintoretto used a large team of apprentices and was known to use unscrupulous means to secure his commissions; both of which made him unpopular.

Tintoretto once described his art as combining the form of Michelangelo with the color of Titian and, indeed, both elements are present in many of his paintings, from his evident fascination with the body in movement to the rich, deep colors that he employed. Tintoretto was commissioned to paint the familiar scene of the Last Supper eight times by various patrons. Here, he has employed an oblique perspective, rather than the traditional frontal one, with the table edge running at an angle to the frame. The scene is infused with drama by the dynamic portrayal of the agitation of the disciples.

GIOVANNI BATTISTA MORONI (C.1525–78)

THE SCULPTOR, ALESSANDRO VITTORIA (1625–1608)

Kunsthistorisches Museum, Gemaeldegalerie, Vienna. Celimage.sa/Lessing Archive

BORN in Bergamo, Moroni moved to Brescia to study with the master Alessandro Moretto (c.1498–1554), whose influence is clear in Moroni's earlier works. The similarity of style between the two is marked and they may have collaborated on several paintings. Like most Renaissance artists, Moroni's earlier works are dominated by religious themes, since many of the wealthiest patrons were key figures in the church.

Moroni's fame, however, was due to his remarkable skill at portraiture. His approach to portrait painting was heavily influenced by Lotto, although he evinces a natural realism that is absent in Lotto's works; conversely, Moroni's work does not include symbolic references, nor does it attempt to create the level of empathy with the sitter that Lotto achieved. Although it was usual for Renaissance artists to choose aristocratic, wealthy subjects, Moroni used working-class subjects in his portraits.

The Sculptor has a stark background, from which the gaze of the subject is riveting. The painting has a distinctly modern feel. It is as sensitive in portrayal as any great nineteenth- or twentieth-century portrait. The use of light and color interweave to offer a powerful and memorable image.

SOFONISBA ANGUISSOLA (C.1532–1625)

SELF-PORTRAIT

Pinacoteca di Brera, Milan. Celimage.sa/Lessing Archive

SOFONISBA Anguissola was born into a noble family in Cremona, one of four artistically talented sisters. During the sixteenth century in Italy there were about 40 female artists, of whom Anguissola was the most successful; her paintings were bought by many great families.

Her talent was recognized at an early age and after her mother died, her liberal father encouraged and supported her, which enabled her to overcome the constraints of sixteenth-century life. For three years she studied in Cremona under Bernardino Campi, then from about 1549 she studied with the Spanish artist Il Sojaro for a further three years. Records of her father's letters to Michelangelo about Anguissola exist; in these he asks the master for a sketch in his own hand for Anguissola to paint. Anguissola's skill was spotted by the Duke of Alba in Spain, and soon her talent at portraiture was rewarded by employment as court painter and lady-in-waiting at the court of Queen Isabel of Spain, where she lived for several years. The self-portrait was a genre in which Anguissola excelled. Here, a youthful Anguissola stares out of the painting, with a hint of a smile lifting the corners of her mouth and wide-open eyes that imply apprehension.

PAOLO VERONESE (1528–88)

THE MARRIAGE FEAST AT CANA

Louvre, Paris. Celimage.sa/Lessing Archive

PAOLO Caliari was born in Verona, hence he was known by the name Veronese. He studied with Antonio Badile while living in Verona, before moving to Venice in about 1553. With Titian and Tintoretto, Veronese dominated the Venetian art scene. His use of color differed from that of other painters of the Venetian school, and hints of his training in Verona can be seen in his distinctive yet harmonious coloring.

Veronese often painted religious scenes, placing them in an incongruous Venetian setting with the saints dressed in finery and jewels. Although he was censored for this decorative element, which some viewed as sacrilegious, it enabled him to portray the splendor of life in the rich and triumphant city-state of Venice.

During the early years of his career in Venice, Veronese painted frescoes for the great architect Sanmicheli. As a result, many of his works convey a lasting impression of the detail of architecture, including *The Marriage Feast at Cana*, where the feast takes place against a magnificent backdrop of sweeping Classical colonnades. The architectural setting intensifies the illusion that the painting is a scene from a play—sixteenth-century theaters often had two such flanking flights of stairs. Veronese has included a self-portrait of himself playing the *viola da braccio*; beside him are fellow artists Titian and Tintoretto.

TITIAN (C.1488–1576)

SELF-PORTRAIT

Prado, Madrid. Celimage.sa/Lessing Archive

OF all the Venetian artists who flourished during the sixteenth century, Titian gained the most enduring prestige and renown; his work influenced his contemporaries and generations of oil painters that succeeded him. Although he lived in Venice for almost all of his adult life, his fame brought him eminent patrons in many countries of Europe.

Born in the Dolomites, Titian moved to Venice as a child. He studied with Giovanni and Gentile Bellini, the founders of the Venetian school. He later studied with Giorgione, completing some of the master's works after his sudden death. Titian's own career was long; he lived into his nineties, creating innovative and impressive art even in his final years. In old age he used his fingers to apply the paint, creating an energy and depth of field that was emulated more than three centuries later by the Impressionists.

Unlike other key artists of the High Renaissance, Titian devoted himself solely to oil painting. His most memorable paintings illustrate religious or mythological scenes but he was also a highly skilled portraitist. This late *Self-Portrait* lacks Titian's usual glorious range of color. Instead, he depicts himself dressed in black against a shady background; only his face stands out, ghostly amid the darkness where the light falls softly onto it.

ANDREA DEL SARTO (1486–1530)

PORTRAIT OF A YOUNG MAN

Uffizi Gallery, Florence. Celimage.sa/Scala Archives

DEL Sarto grew up in Florence, which was then the center of an artistic melting pot. His training was with Piero di Cosimo (c.1462–c.1521), and then he set up a studio with the painter Francesco Franciabigio (c.1482–1525). He also worked with Jacopo Sansovino (1486–1570), with whom he became great friends and occasionally collaborated.

In c.1517 he married a young widow, Lucrezia, of whom he made several portraits. Some time in 1518–19 he left Florence for the French court of Francis I at Fontainebleau, where he was a great success. He returned to Florence after entreaties from Lucrezia, where he was elected to the prestigious Companies of San Luca and San Sebastiano. Despite his avowed intentions to return to France, he remained in Italy, becoming one of Florence's most respected artists.

Although the vast majority of Del Sarto's work is religious, he painted several portraits, including *Portrait of a Young Man*, and an occasional self-portrait. His work is deeply moving: the eyes of the sitter, like those in his *Christ Redeemer* (1515–16), are haunting in their intensity. The eyes of the young man seem to look directly at the viewer, holding them spellbound.

JACOPO DA PONTORMO (1494–1556)

THE VIRGIN WITH SAINT ANNE AND FOUR SAINTS (PETER, SEBASTIAN, BENEDICT, AND THE GOOD MALEFACTOR)

Louvre, Paris. Celimage.sa/Lessing Archive

PONTORMO, whose real name was Jacopo Carucci, adopted the name of the city of his birth in Italy. As a young man, he moved from his home town to Florence and undertook artistic training under Mannerist master Andrea del Sarto. Through Del Sarto, Pontormo came into contact with Jacopo Sansovino, as well as moving within the same circles as the elderly Leonardo da Vinci and Piero di Cosimo (c. 1462–c. 1521). His work was also influenced by Michelangelo and Albrecht Dürer (1471–1528).

As an associate of Del Sarto, Pontormo came to the attention of the Medici Grand Duke, Cosimo I (1519–74), who commissioned him to decorate one of his villas with frescoes; he also worked on Lorenzo de' Medici's villa at Poggia a Caiano, as well as the decorations of the Chiostro Grande in Florence's Medici Chapel in preparation for a state visit by Pope Leo X (1475–1521).

Saint Anne is revered in Florence and this painting marked the destination of a procession celebrating the city's liberation from tyranny.

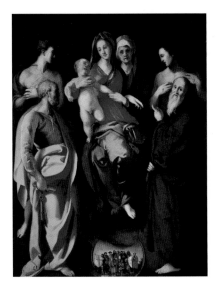

CORREGGIO (C.1490–1534)

NOLI ME TANGERE

Prado, Madrid. Celimage.sa/Lessing Archive

CORREGGIO, whose real name was Antonio Allegri, was born in Correggio, Italy. For most of his life he worked in and around Parma, in an artistic style that bordered High Renaissance and Mannerism. He was strongly influenced by Andrea Mantegna, and followed the older artist's example in painting church domes with a *sotto in sù* effect to create the illusion that the subjects of the painting were floating freely in mid-air. The result is an extremely lifelike and realistic effect, as though the scene is actually taking place above our heads. Correggio achieved this wonderful effect after intensive study of the effects of light and shadow; a superb example of his *sotto in sù* work can be seen in the *Assumption* (1526–30) at Parma Cathedral.

Correggio also produced mythological paintings, such as the *Loves of Jupiter* series (c.1530–33). His work reveals an indebtedness to Raphael, da Vinci and Michelangelo. His mastery of light can be seen in the glowering sky of *Noli Me Tangere*, which was painted at the end of his life. Correggio's work was hugely influential on the Baroque movement and on the work of Bernini (1598–1680) and Parmigianino (1503–40).

PARMIGIANINO (1503–40)

MADONNA WITH THE LONG NECK

Uffizi Gallery, Florence. Celimage.sa/Lessing Archive

GIROLAMO Francesco Maria Mazzola was nicknamed "Parmigianino" after his home town of Parma in Italy. In 1524 he traveled to Rome, although German occupation in 1527 saw him fleeing from imprisonment to the safety of Bologna. From there he returned to Parma in 1531. As well as oils, Parmigianino produced engravings and frescoes, decorating churches in the cities of Rome, Bologna, and Parma.

Parmigianino was a pupil of Correggio, and was also influenced by Raphael and Michelangelo, although he developed a unique style. His works were renowned for their eroticism, unusual perspective, heightened imagination, and elongation of the human figure. The latter can be seen in *The Madonna with the Long Neck*, which caused a contemporary uproar. Parmigianino's intention was to emphasize the Madonna's beauty by giving her an elongated neck—a sign of great beauty and of sexual availability.

Toward the end of his short life, Parmigianino became obsessed with alchemy, a fixation that seems to have heralded his insanity. He was imprisoned for breach of contract when he left the fresco at Santa Maria della Steccata in Parma unfinished. He died aged just 37.

AGNOLO BRONZINO (1503–72)

ELEANORA OF TOLEDO AND HER SON

Uffizi Gallery, Florence. Celimage.sa/Lessing Archive

AGNOLO Bronzino was one of the first generation of Mannerists. He became a court painter and favorite of Duke Cosimo I de' Medici (1519–74— a generous patron of the arts who also furthered the careers of Benvenuto Cellini (1500–71) and Giorgio Vasari (1511–74).

Bronzino was well known as a portrait painter. This portrait is of Cosimo de' Medici's wife, Eleanora, and their son Giovanni de' Medici, one of their eight children. The pattern on Eleanora's dress is exquisitely detailed, as is her hair decoration and the embroidery of Giovanni's collar and cuffs. The white material of the dress is rendered faithfully, gleaming and occasionally dappled by the shadow of its folds. The inscrutable expressions on the faces of both subjects are characteristic of Bronzino's portrait work, which did not seek to reveal the character of the sitters. Instead, he used clarity of color and a depiction of the richness of the clothes to denote their elevated social status. This, coupled with his obvious talent and fashionable connections, made Bronzino a popular and much sought-after portraitist.

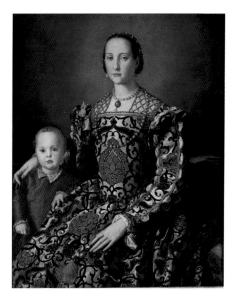

GIAMBOLOGNA (1529–1608)

THE RAPE OF THE SABINE WOMEN

Museo Bargello, Florence. Celimage.sa/Scala Archives

GIAMBOLOGNA, the best known and most important Mannerist sculptor was Flemish by birth but relocated to Italy. After initial training in the Netherlands, between c.1545 and 1550, he moved to Rome, where he lived for two years before settling permanently in Florence. Here he was patronized by the Medici ruler Ferdinando I (1549–1609), who commissioned Giambologna to sculpt an enormous equestrian statue of Grand Duke Cosimo I (1519–74), which set a precedent for equestrian-style statues throughout Europe.

Giambologna worked in marble and bronze. His works range in size from small bronzes, such as *Mercury* (c.1565), now in the Bargello, Florence, to the monumental piece that sealed his reputation, *Neptune's Fountain* (1566), in Bologna.

His sculptures were ground-breaking for their apparent ability to defy the laws of gravity and in their portrayal of movement, as seen in *The Rape of the Sabine Women*. The sculpture is much admired for its fluidity and anatomical accuracy, from the cowering man at the base to the pinnacle of the woman's outstretched hand.

DOMENIKOS THEOTOCOPOULOS
"EL GRECO" (1541–1614)

THE BURIAL OF COUNT ORGAZ

Church of Saint Thomas, Toledo. Celimage.sa / Lessing Archive

DOMENIKOS Theotocopoulos was born in Crete. At the age of 19 he traveled to Italy, spending time in Venice—Crete was currently under Venetian rule—and Rome. In the mid-1570s he moved to Toledo in Spain, where he remained. It was in Toledo that he was given the name "El Greco," "the Greek," by which he is still known. He resisted the nickname, however, signing his paintings with his real name, in Greek.

El Greco's early work was Byzantine in style, but he soon became absorbed by the Mannerist style during his protracted sojourn in Spain, and is known as "the last Mannerist painter." His works consisted mainly of religious paintings and portraits, such as *Fra Felix Hortensio Paracivino* (c.1605), although he also painted a number of landscapes and one mythological painting: the splendid *Laocoön* (c.1610). El Greco was also an architect and sculptor.

The Burial of Count Orgaz is based on a legend that dates back to 1323: the count was a deeply religious and charitable man, of such piety that Saints Augustine and Stephen materialized at his funeral and lowered his body to its resting place.

ALBRECHT DÜRER (1471–1528)

SELF-PORTRAIT

Prado, Madrid. Celimage.sa/Lessing Archive

NORTHERN Renaissance art is commonly viewed as secondary to that of Renaissance Italy, with the notable exception of German artist Albrecht Dürer. He had magnificent technical abilities, synthesizing Italian and Northern traditions in a unique and much-imitated style that brought him recognition even in Italy. In 1496 Dürer visited Venice, meeting Gentile Bellini, who greatly influenced his painting. He visited Italy once again in 1505–07, assimilating the many artistic and humanist innovations of the Renaissance.

Dürer's fame spread with his engravings and woodcuts, as evidenced by his celebrated book *The Apocalypse* (1498). Book illustrations were becoming increasingly popular and, with Dürer's remarkable achievements, more skillfully executed than ever. Many of Dürer's letters, annotations, and theories on anatomy and perspective survive. They reveal an intelligent, educated man, ever curious about the world around him. Dürer helped to raise the profile of artists in Germany.

Dürer painted this self-portrait when he was 26. He holds a strikingly confident pose and his countenance basks in the light filtering through the open window. The artist invests himself with an air of nobility.

LUCAS CRANACH THE ELDER (1472–1553)

VENUS AND AMOR

Galleria Borghese, Rome. Celimage.sa/Lessing Archive

LUCAS Cranach the Elder (he had two sons) was born in Kronach, southern Germany. He learnt painting and engraving skills from his father. Cranach was a friend and supporter of the religious reformer Martin Luther (1483–1546) and, greatly influenced by Dürer's work, he produced several propaganda woodcuts for the Protestant cause.

Cranach traveled to Vienna in about 1501. The landscape work he produced here created a lasting impression, contributing to the foundation of the Danube School—a group that focused on the importance of landscape painting, particularly of background landscapes used to reflect the emotions or actions of the people portrayed. From 1508 Cranach worked as a court painter for Frederick the Wise, Elector of Saxony, at Wittenberg. Many of his finest portraits were of court subjects; his portraits were intensely detailed and highly decorative, full of color and character.

Venus and Amor is typical of the paintings for which Cranach is chiefly remembered, in both style and content. Like Cranach's other female nudes, this highly stylized Venus is oddly disproportionate (for reasons of propriety, female models were not used at this time) and has an unearthly quality.

HANS HOLBEIN THE YOUNGER (C.1497–1543)

THE AMBASSADORS

The National Gallery, London. Celimage.sa/Lessing Archive

THE German artist Hans Holbein the Younger worked in his father's workshop in Augsburg before moving to Basel, Switzerland, in 1514, where he gained recognition for his book illustrations, most notably the illustration of the Luther Bible in 1522. Luther's Reformation movement had brought troubled times to Europe, influencing Holbein's decision to move to England in 1526 in search of greater prosperity.

In England, Holbein worked for the high-ranking Sir Thomas More (1478–1535), and his second visit in 1532 led to a portrait commission from King Henry VIII. By 1536 he was working for the King as a painter and costume and jewelry designer. His meticulously detailed court portraits, especially those of the king, secured Holbein's already esteemed reputation. *The Ambassadors* shows the French ambassador on the left, with a friend. They are surrounded by objects that illustrate their social standing and wealth, but the distorted shape of the skull beneath them (which achieves correct perspective when viewed from a side angle) is an indicator of their mortality. *The Ambassadors* contains a wealth of precise and minute detail, a typical feature of Northern Renaissance art that began with Jan van Eyck.

NICHOLAS HILLIARD (C.1547–1619)

SIR WALTER RALEIGH (1552–1618)

National Portrait Gallery, London. Courtesy of Edimedia

NICHOLAS Hilliard was the first English-born painter about whom any significant historical facts were recorded. He was born in Exeter and was trained by his father as a goldsmith, but by the age of 13 was showing remarkable flair for miniature painting. By 1569 Hilliard had become a painter of portraits at the court of Queen Elizabeth I (1558–1603).

While at court, Hilliard continued to make use of his training as a goldsmith, designing the Queen's second Great Seal in 1584. However, his main recognition came from his skill at painting miniatures, or "limners," as they were called. By the late sixteenth century the miniature had become a fashionable item and was often worn as jewelry, especially in the royal courts of England and France. Hilliard quoted one of his influences as Holbein the Younger, whose intricately detailed paintings must have yielded much for him to study.

Sir Walter Raleigh, English explorer, courtier, and poet, was a controversial figure of the Elizabethan Age, renowned for his wit. In this portrait, his expression and attire suggest a man of wealth and stature. Here, Raleigh embodies the Elizabethan values of opulence and power.

JOACHIM PATENIER (C.1485–1524)

CHARON CROSSING THE RIVER STYX

Prado, Madrid. Celimage.sa/Scala Archives

JOACHIM Patenier was born in France but by 1515 had registered as a master in the city of Antwerp. He was a friend of the great German artist Albrecht Dürer, whose detailed prints of dark subjects evidently impressed Patenier, for his dramatic paintings often simulate the themes found in Dürer's work.

Patenier's use of landscape changed the direction of Flemish art. During the Renaissance, landscape was increasingly used as the background of a painted scene, particularly in portraits, such as Leonardo da Vinci's *Mona Lisa* (1503). The inclusion of landscape became more prominent in works such as Giorgione's *The Tempest* (c.1508). However, in Patenier's work the landscape eclipsed the subject to become the primary focus. Later artists such as Pieter Bruegel (1525–69) were influenced by Patenier's work, and landscapes became dominant in sixteenth-century Flemish art.

In *Charon Crossing the River Styx* the narrative is overshadowed by the compelling landscape that Patenier has invented. Charon is seen in his boat moving toward the viewer across an unearthly-colored sea. On his right are the welcoming Elysian Fields, on his left the darkly burning fires of Hell. In his fantastic, supernatural landscape, Patenier combines the Gothic tradition with the skills of a High Renaissance painter.

Northern Landscape

PIETER BRUEGEL THE ELDER (C.1525–69)

THE TOWER OF BABEL

Künsthistorisches Museum, Vienna. Celimage.sa/Lessing Archive

NAMED after his home village in the Netherlands, Pieter Bruegel founded a dynasty of painters. Alongside Dürer, he was the most outstanding Northern European Renaissance artist. Bruegel did not try to assimilate the artistic ideals of the Italian Renaissance— the Classical imagery or the harmonious balance and idealized beauty. Instead his artistic direction owes more to his compatriots Bosch (c.1450–1516) and Patenier. From Bosch, Bruegel took elements of the Gothic and the fantastical to incorporate into his paintings while he followed Patenier's lead in his keen observation of landscape.

Bruegel's portrayals of a seasonally changing landscape usually contained groups of detailed figures, shown hunting, skating across frozen rivers, or stumbling through the landscape in drunken festivity. The landscape dominates all these works and the inclusion of tiny figures implies the triviality of man as he battles against the forces of nature. In several paintings he depicted scenes of peasant life; his interest in the lower classes (to which he did not belong) earned him the nickname "Peasant Bruegel."

Bruegel often took a moral viewpoint in his work, and here retells the biblical story of the Tower of Babel: God's devastation of a city for its attempt to build a tower that reached to heaven.

JAN BRUEGEL THE ELDER (1568–1625)

FLOWERS IN A VASE

Civic Museum, Cremona. Celimage.sa/Scala Archives

JAN Bruegel the Elder was the son of Pieter Bruegel the Elder. Several other members of the Bruegel family were painters, but only Jan found a level of recognition approaching that of his father. His sons also followed the family tradition by becoming artists.

Like his father, Jan traveled in Italy, where he became a member of the prestigious Guild of Rome. He showed great skill in miniature details and so was commissioned to make many cabinet paintings. Jan also collaborated with a number of other painters, including Peter Paul Rubens (1577–1640).

However, it was Jan Bruegel's landscapes that brought him lasting recognition, intensifying the existing tradition of Dutch landscape painting in the seventeenth century. Scenes such as the *Garden of Eden* (c.1602), filled with naturalistic details in a lush profusion of flora and fauna, are typical.

Jan was given the nickname "Velvet Bruegel" because of the high level of finish employed in his paintings. Despite his success with landscapes, he was regarded as the greatest flower painter of his day, and produced exquisite still life studies such as *Flowers in a Vase*, in which his consummate skill in rendering different textures and capturing the light is evident.

THE DELIGHTS OF WINTER

Mauritshuis, The Hague. Celimage.sa/Scala Archives

THE Dutch landscape painter Heindrick Avercamp is believed to have been deaf and was known as "the mute of Kampen." He spent most of his life in Kampen, a small town set beside a canal in the province of Zuider Zee in the north of Holland. From his style of painting, it is likely that at some time he trained with David Vinckboons (1576–1632) of the Bruegel school. Throughout his career, Avercamp's style did not change. Neither did his subject matter alter greatly—a wintry landscape set beside a frozen canal or river, with minute figures scurrying around. The apparent restriction in his range could be explained by Avercamp's lack of contact with other artists in the major artistic centers that were blossoming elsewhere in the Netherlands.

Avercamp's paintings show us captured moments of time in a small, seventeenth-century Dutch town. His wintry scenes are busy with many small figures of townspeople in various pursuits, such as fishing, skating, playing golf, or curling on the ice. Here, the distant figures are minuscule, painted with the same intense detail as a miniature. Avercamp was following a long tradition in Northern European art of paying close attention to small details to enhance the overall effect of the picture.

GIUSEPPE ARCIMBOLDO (1527–93)

SPRING ALLEGORY

Louvre, Paris. Celimage.sa/Lessing Archive

ARCIMBOLDO, the son of a painter, was born in Milan to a well-connected family. He began his career making stained-glass windows and designing frescoes as well as painting; in later years he concentrated solely on the latter. In 1562, Arcimboldo traveled to Vienna to the Habsburg court of Ferdinand I. He was to become a court favorite, spending more of his life in the Habsburg Empire than in his native country. He returned to Milan for the last decade of his life.

Grotesque allegories such as *Spring Allegory* brought Arcimboldo much acclaim in his lifetime, and were often imitated. The original meaning of the term "grotesque," as applied to art, is a picture whose subject is created from other forms, in this case fruit, vegetables, and flowers. After his death, Arcimboldo's popularity faded and his subject matter was treated with derision. It was not until the twentieth century, and the development of Surrealism, that his fame was revived. Salvador Dalí (1904–89), in particular, was strongly influenced by Arcimboldo.

Spring Allegory forms part of Arcimboldo's "Four Seasons" series. His use of color is precise and accurate, as is his brushwork.

ANNIBALE CARRACCI (1560–1609)

CHRIST AND THE SAMARITAN WOMAN

Pinacoteca di Brera, Milan. Celimage.sa/Lessing Archive

ANNIBALE Carracci was the younger brother of Agostino Carracci (1557–1602) and the cousin of Lodovico Carracci (1555–1619). The trio set up one of the most successful studios of their time, exporting works across Europe. Annibale is generally considered the most talented of the three, but together the group combined formidable artistry and business acumen.

Together with his brother Agostino, and cousin Lodovico, Carracci founded the Accademia degli Incamminati (Academy of the Progressives) in Bologna. Here, he and his fellow artists focused on naturalism. They worked largely from life with models, which became the subject of keen artistic observation. Between 1597 and 1601, Carracci worked on the gallery ceiling of the Palazzo Farnese in Rome. Pictures such as *Domine, Quo Vadis?* (c.1602) reveal a striking economy in figure composition. Carracci was ultimately to influence the French artist, Poussin, and through him, the whole language of gesture in painting. In his last years, Carracci was overcome by depression and effectively stopped painting. He contracted a form of paralysis in 1605, and died in Rome in 1609. He was buried near Raphael in the Pantheon at Rome.

Christ and the Samaritan Woman is a work of dramatic power, a moving exploration of its subject.

MICHELANGELO MERISI DA CARAVAGGIO
(1571–1610)

SUPPER AT EMMAUS

Pinacoteca di Brera, Milan. Celimage.sa/Lessing Archive

CARAVAGGIO'S early education was undertaken in Lombardy, under the tutelage of Simone Peterzano, who had studied under Titian (c.1487–1576). Around 1592, Caravaggio left Lombardy for Rome, seeking artistic fame. He began his career in Rome as a painter of portraits, as well as perfecting still life and historical painting.

Caravaggio spent much of his life traveling in Europe—partly because he had an incendiary temper which often got him into trouble. On more than one occasion he was forced to move on after becoming involved in some brawl or other; in 1606 he fled Rome in fear of his life after a gambling disagreement ended in his adversary's death.

By 1600 he had become increasingly interested in religious subjects. In *Supper at Emmaus*, he uses the techniques developed in his earlier work. The penetrating study of Jesus as an ordinary man is central to the painting, while the shocked faces and gestures of the disciples are portrayed with startling, harrowing immediacy by Caravaggio's skilled use of chiaroscuro (light and shade). The fruit and bread are painted as carefully as in a still life.

Caravaggio died in prison of a fever—ironically after being arrested for a crime that he did not commit.

ARTEMISIA GENTILESCHI (1597–C.1652)

JUDITH SLAYING HOLOFERNES

Uffizi Gallery, Florence. Celimage.sa/Lessing Archive

ARTEMISIA was the daughter of wealthy Orazio Gentileschi (1563–c.1639), a Mannerist painter patronized by the Florentine Medicis and the Duke of Buckingham in England. Orazio taught his daughter to paint directly onto the canvas, and their styles are extremely similar. Artemisia was influenced by Mannerism, in particular by Bronzino (1503–72) and Pontormo (1494–1556). Orazio hired painter Agostino Tassi to assist in the education of his daughter. In 1611, Tassi raped Artemisia, after which he was arrested, tried publicly, and subsequently imprisoned. Artemisia then married and moved to Florence.

It seems likely that Artemisia chose the theme of *Judith Slaying Holofernes* as a result of her painful experience: in the painting, Holofernes clearly intends to rape Judith, who can be seen exacting her revenge. Artemisia returned to the theme in around 1625, with another jubilant portrayal of a strong, determined woman in *Judith and her Maidservant with the Head of Holofernes*.

Artemisia was remarkable for being the only female artist in Italy to be taken seriously at this time. Toward the end of her life she became the first woman to gain admittance to the Accademia del Disegno in Florence.

GUIDO RENI (1575–1642)

SAINT SEBASTIAN

Museo del Prado, Madrid. Celimage.sa/Lessing Archive

RENI was a celebrated figure in his own lifetime. When his tutor Lodovico Carracci (1555–1619) died, Reni took over his studio, inheriting an already secured fortune and reputation. Works of art from Carracci's studio had long been in demand throughout Europe, and this continued under Reni.

Reni took much of his inspiration from Caravaggio (1571–1610) and Raphael (1483–1520); however, the overriding influence on his work was his quest for beauty and perfection. He took great pains to recreate the colors of his subject exactly and to reproduce the facial idiosyncracies of his models. These aesthetic values also affected his personal life; contemporary reports survive of his impeccable attire and moral beliefs.

The facial expression of Saint Sebastian recalls Reni's impassioned *Head of Christ* (c. 1640). Saint Sebastian was a favorite subject of the Renaissance and his popularity continued in the ensuing centuries. Other than the method of his death by arrow, very little is known about him, although various legends abound. He was particularly popular with Italian artists because he was believed to have been a native of Milan who was martyred in Rome. His body is reputed to be buried beneath the Appian Way.

PIETRO DA CORTONA (1596–1669)

THE BATTLE OF ALEXANDER AGAINST
KING DARIUS I

Pinacoteca Capitolina, Rome. Celimage.sa/Lessing Archive

PIETRO da Cortona was born Pietro Berettini, but was better known by the name of his birthplace, Cortona. He moved to Florence in 1613, where he was greatly influenced by the work of Michelangelo (1475–1564). Cortona is credited with the invention of the High Baroque style of ceiling painting, a technique that was to bring him great fame within his lifetime. Cortona was an accomplished painter in oils and an architect. His architectural works include the churches of Santa Maria della Pace (1656–57) and Santi Martina e Luca (1635) in Rome.

The Battle of Alexander against King Darius I is an epic treatment of a popular heroic theme. It is clearly a Baroque work, with a tumult of detail and activity. In this final scene from the battle between Greek and Persian forces the two great protagonists of the war are pitted against each other. Darius (on the right) prepares to flee the battlefield. Alexander emerges as a powerful superstar, who youthfully charges toward his foe. He is depicted as fearless and determined to prevail.

NICOLAS POUSSIN (1594–1665)

ET IN ARCADIA EGO

NICOLAS Poussin was arguably the most influential French painter of the seventeenth century. His life was spent alternating between France and Rome, where he sought inspiration in rural areas outside the city.

Poussin's work was influenced by that of Raphael, among others. He was unhappy at first with the excesses of the Baroque style, preferring to draw inspiration from the Mannerists, but his individual Classical style became more empathetic with the Baroque style as his career progressed. Poussin was also influenced by literature. Many of his works illustrate Greek or Roman myths and scenes from the Old Testament, such as *The Worship of the Golden Calf* (c.1635) and *The Gathering of the Manna* (1639).

Scenes of an Arcadian idyll were especially popular subjects for Poussin. Here, a group of shepherds are attempting to decipher the words "Et in Arcadia Ego" inscribed on the tomb in the center of the painting. The words indicate the presence of death even in the most idyllic surroundings.

Baroque

CLAUDE LORRAIN (CLAUDE GELLÉE) (C.1600–82)

THE EMBARKATION OF SAINT URSULA

The National Gallery, London. Celimage.sa/Lessing Archive

CLAUDE Lorrain (born Claude Gellée) left his native France at the age of 14 and traveled to Italy, where he settled in Rome. He specialized in the genre of landscape painting, and showed little interest in figure work. In his paintings the people are vastly overshadowed by the landscape, as in *The Embarkation of Saint Ursula* and *Landscape with Cephalus and Procris Reunited by Diana* (1645).

Lorrain often painted in the open air and was entranced by the idea of Arcadia. He reputedly spent months at a time living among shepherds and tramps to gain the inspiration for his paintings. His landscapes adhere closely to a pastoral ideal, in which people constitute only a small part of a much greater whole. Lorrain often employed studio assistants to paint in the people in his works, while he concerned himself solely with the landscape.

Here Saint Ursula is almost insignificant, despite such prominence in the title. The legend tells of a British princess who fled her father's house to avoid marrying against her will. She took 11,000 maids with her and, collectively, they became known as the Virgin Martyrs. Ursula and her maids visited Rome to pay allegiance to the Pope but, on the return journey from Rome, they were martyred by a horde of Huns in Cologne.

GIANLORENZO BERNINI (1598–1680)

ECSTASY OF SAINT TERESA OF ÁVILA

Santa Maria della Vittoria, Rome. Celimage.sa/Lessing Archive

GIANLORENZO Bernini— sculptor, painter, designer, and architect—was the son of a highly accomplished Mannerist sculptor, Pietro Bernini (1562–1629). Although influenced by his father's work, Gianlorenzo was firmly of his own era and was instrumental in the move from Mannerism to Baroque art. It is largely due to the prevalence of his works in Rome that the city has such a prominently Baroque style.

His surviving work in Rome includes Piazza Navona's *Fountain of the Four Rivers* (1648–51) and several aspects of Saint Peter's Basilica in the Vatican. Bernini's ability to make solid marble appear as flowing drapery, as well as his obvious skill in facial portraiture, was unsurpassed.

Saint Teresa is one of Bernini's most famous works. It is set in the fantastically ornate marble surroundings of the Cornaro Chapel, and is a focal point for visitors to the church of Santa Maria della Vittoria in Rome. Teresa was a mystic, nun, and religious reformer who lived between 1515 and 1582. The sculpture depicts one of her famous ecstasies, in which God sends an arrow of golden flame into her heart. The arrow in the angel's hand is accentuated by the golden rods behind and above the marble figures.

JUSEPE DE RIBERA (1591–1652)

SAINT PAUL THE HERMIT

Louvre, Paris. Celimage.sa/Lessing Archive

IN 1616, Jusepe de Ribera— also known as José de Ribera and "lo Spagnoletto" (the little Spaniard)—moved from his native Spain to Naples, in Italy, which was then under Spanish rule. He studied Caravaggio (1571–1610) and Correggio, and his early work, in particular, shows their influence in the use of chiaroscuro. Ribera went on to develop his own artistic style, which often included depictions of harsh social realism and portrayals of religious piety and suffering.

De Ribera's subjects usually dealt with martyrdom and other religious themes. *Saint Paul the Hermit* is evocative of his earlier paintings, such as *The Martyrdom of Saint Bartholomew* (c.1630), in its somber realism. The wasting muscles, sagging skin, and heavily lined face predicate the hastening end of Saint Paul's life. It is a poignant portrayal of a saint who is more usually represented by his religious fervor and passion. The rushes he wears, the color and texture of which seem to meld with the dirt beneath him, intimate that he is soon to be part of the earth. The skull at the bottom left of the painting is a common artistic metaphor indicating human mortality.

DIEGO RODRÍGUEZ DE SILVA Y VELÁZQUEZ
(1599–1660)

LAS MENINAS OR THE FAMILY OF PHILIP IV

Prado, Madrid. Celimage.sa/Lessing Archive

VELÁZQUEZ was born in Seville and moved to Madrid in 1622. He visited Italy several times, but always returned to Madrid, establishing himself as the foremost artist of the Spanish School. He was influenced by Titian (c.1487–1576), Tintoretto (1518–94), and Veronese (c.1528–88); he was also great friends with Rubens (1577–1640).

Although Velázquez painted mainly portraits after his royal appointment, he remained interested in other genres; the harsh realities of everyday life, for example, are encapsulated in his early works *The Water Carrier of Seville* (c.1618)). The artist was a favorite of the Spanish King Philip IV, who appointed him as court painter when Velázquez was still only 24. *Las Meninas* not only shows the royal family (Philip and his wife are reflected in the mirror from the artist's canvas), but also Velázquez himself, apparently looking beyond his easel toward the viewer.

The central child in the portrait is the Infanta Margarita, attended by all her maids. Note the female dwarf to the right of the picture. Dwarfs were a common theme in Velázquez's paintings, as many were employed in Philip's household as entertainers.

FRANCISCO DE ZURBARÁN (1598–1664)

THE APOSTLE SAINT ANDREW

Museum of Fine Arts, Budapest. Celimage.sa/Lessing Archive

ZURBARÁN was a painter of the Spanish School and, through Velázquez's recommendation, was employed as a court painter for King Philip IV in Madrid: in the 1630s, he decorated Philip's new palace there. Despite this prestigious commission, he spent most of his life in Seville, where he was honored as one of the city's "official" painters.

Zurbaran's oeuvre spanned mythologies, still-life painting, and historical scenes. The bulk of his work, however, comprised portraits and religious works—*The Apostle Saint Andrew* encompasses both genres.

The Apostle Andrew was born at Bethsaida near the Sea of Galilee. He grew up a fisherman. This painting depicts the saint wearing the brown habit of the monks of the Franciscan order.

BARTOLOMÉ ESTEBAN MURILLO (1618–82)

LA NAISSANCE DE LA VIERGE
(BIRTH OF SAINT MARY)

Louvre, Paris. Celimage.sa/Lessing Archive

UNUSUALLY for an artist, Murillo found fame in his own lifetime. In his twenties, he created a series of paintings (1645–46) for the Franciscan friary in his native Seville, which was an important artistic center at this time. The 11 paintings depicting Franciscan saints brought him to the attention of the art establishment, and led to many commissions. Murillo became renowned for his religious and sentimental scenes—themes guaranteed to be popular with the contemporary art-buying public—and is known to have painted the occasional society portrait.

Murillo's importance in Seville reached its pinnacle when he helped to set up an Academy of Art—and was appointed its first president. His death in 1682—after a fall from scaffolding while working on a large commission—did not signal the end of his fame. He has continued to be revered, both in Spain and abroad, during the ensuing centuries.

La Naissance de la Vierge is a fine example of Murillo's technique of applying delicate brushstrokes to compose his works. He always chose models with empathetic faces for his paintings—as in *Beggar Boys Throwing Dice* (c.1670), for example—and imbued his compositions with an emotion that retains its significance for the modern-day viewer.

SIR PETER PAUL RUBENS (1577–1640)

THE RAPE OF DEIDAMIA

Prado, Madrid. Celimage.sa/Lessing Archive

FLEMISH painter Rubens received a classical education, and his travels in Italy at the beginning of the seventeenth century furthered his interest in the work of the Renaissance and Venetian masters. He was also a successful and well-respected ambassador, serving diplomatic assignments in Spain, France, England, and Holland. He was knighted for his efforts by Charles I in 1630.

Rubens was the leading figure of the Flemish Baroque school. His subjects included religious and mythological scenes as well as hunting scenes and portraits; he excelled in all these genres. His work is characterized by a sense of drama typical of the Baroque period, suffused with energetic movement, naturalistic light, and glowing colors.

Obviously inspired by his visits to Italy, Rubens' sumptuous and bold colors emulate those of the great Venetian master Titian (c.1488–1576). The influence of another Italian master, Michelangelo (1475–1564), is evident in the *Rape of Deidamia*. The bodies are painted with the same muscular, sculptural quality as the prophets in Michelangelo's frescoes for the Sistine Chapel (1508–12). This piece emphasizes Rubens's unequalled mastery in the portrayal of real skin and luxurious cloth.

Flemish Baroque

FRANS HALS (C.1582–1666)

RENÉ DESCARTES

Louvre, Paris. Celimage.sa / Lessing Archive

FRANS Hals lived in Haarlem for most of his life. In 1616 he found fame with a group portrait of Dutch civic guards, and many portrait commissions followed. Today Hals's portraits, with an expressive energy partly derived from his furious brushwork, are viewed as second only to Rembrandt's (1606–69). Unusually for an artist of the Baroque period, Hals's technique is spontaneous and instinctive; he pays scant attention to finish and fine detail, preferring to capture a fleeting moment.

Hals was one of the original pioneers of the *alla prima* technique of painting directly onto the canvas, which, much later, earned the admiration of the Impressionists. His work was not highly regarded during his lifetime and he died in poverty, largely unknown. Possibly because of Hals's brusque style of painting and often jovial eye, his commissions declined, even though his later works show a greater sobriety and darker colors.

Hals animated the faces of his models with particular expressions, giving the viewer a superficial glimpse of the person at a certain moment. His poses were informal and often included an expressive gesture.

Flemish Baroque

SIR ANTHONY VAN DYCK (1599–1641)

CHARLES I OF ENGLAND

Prado, Madrid. Celimage.sa/Scala Archives

VAN Dyck was born in Antwerp, northern Belgium. He was artistically precocious and was apprenticed by the age of ten. By the age of 17, he had his own studio. From 1618 to 1621 he was chief assistant to Rubens, who taught van Dyck to refine his already accomplished use of paint so that, by the 1620s, his painting style had become precise and fluent.

Van Dyck produced mythological and religious paintings in addition to his many court portraits, but it was in the latter that he excelled. Van Dyck's portrait style, while influenced by Rubens and Titian, is essentially an expression of his own interpretation of the essence of aristocratic blood; the sitters appear aloof and superior, with an other-worldly aura.

The artist moved to London in 1632, where he was knighted by King Charles I (1600–49) and became portrait artist at his court. Van Dyck painted many portraits of the king, showing him in various poses that were intended to indicate different facets of his sovereignty. Here, Charles is in warrior pose, wearing full armor and seated on a charger. The background landscape is suitably atmospheric, with an evening light that enhances the glowing colors of the horse and the sheen of the metal armor.

JACOB VAN RUISDAEL (1628–82)

THE LANDING STAGE

Louvre, Paris. Celimage.sa/Lessing Archive

CONSIDERED the greatest of the seventeenth-century Dutch landscape painters, Jacob van Ruisdael was born in Haarlem into a family of landscape painters. He was probably taught to paint by his father and uncle. During the 1650s van Ruisdael traveled around Holland and into northern Germany; these travels furnished him with a wealth of images to recreate.

He painted every aspect of the Dutch landscape, from canals and windmills to villages, cityscapes and mountains. His expressive depictions of the beauty of nature revitalized the landscape genre and inspired later Romantic painters.

Van Ruisdael's paintings often have a note of melancholy, portraying scenes of isolated splendor; crumbling buildings, fallen trees, and other objects of decay increase this perception. The artist shows the dramatic majesty of nature while acknowledging its destructive potential. Although most of his paintings spring from reality, van Ruisdael also constructed images of his own invention.

The use of light and shade was an essential ingredient in his atmospheric, emotionally intense landscapes. Van Ruisdael would often focus on one prominent feature in the landscape, like an oak tree, surrounding it with a panorama of details. He would use strong light-dark contrasts and contours, as seen in the gentle yet central focus upon the trees in *The Landing Stage*.

Flemish Baroque

JAN STEEN (1625–79)

FARMERS PLAYING AT SKITTLES

Künsthistorisches Museum, Gemaeldegalerie, Vienna. Celimage.sa/Lessing Archive

STEEN was born in Leiden but moved frequently, working in many Dutch towns including the Hague, Delft, and Haarlem. He studied with Jan van Goyen (1596–1656), whose daughter he married in 1649. His father was a brewer, and in 1654, when it became impossible to live on his meager artist's income, he also became an innkeeper. He did not gain wide recognition in his own lifetime and hundreds of unsold paintings were found after his death.

Steen is mainly known for his scenes of everyday life (genre paintings), many of which illustrate morals, following a tradition set by Bruegel and Bosch. These paintings show the artist's lively sense of humor and irony; he often included portraits of himself in various guises. The incidental details and smaller tableaux taking place behind and around the initial viewpoint are a particular feature of Steen's paintings.

In *Farmers Playing at Skittles*, Steen displays his mastery of color. Like many of his paintings, the scene is one of leisure and merriment. This jovial attitude to his subject matter, possibly a result of his work as an innkeeper, has meant that Steen is not taken as seriously as his work merits.

Flemish Baroque

CAREL FABRITIUS (1622–54)

THE GOLDFINCH

Mauritshuis, The Hague. Celimage.sa/Scala Archives

CAREL Pietersz, known as Fabritius, was born near Amsterdam. In the 1640s he and his brother studied with Rembrandt (1606–69). Carel was Rembrandt's most outstanding apprentice and is regarded by art historians as the link between Rembrandt and Vermeer (1632–75).

Fabritius settled in Delft in 1650, cofounding the Delft School of painting, of which Vermeer later became the leading exponent. He died tragically early, in the 1654 gunpowder explosion in Delft. Much of his work was destroyed with him; only about a dozen of his paintings survive.

With his move to Delft, Fabritius turned away from the historical narratives favored by his master, instead moving toward portraits, still life, and the seventeenth-century Dutch tradition of genre painting, in which he depicted scenes from the lives of ordinary people.

The Goldfinch is Fabritius's most popular painting. In it he explores the tonal implications of placing a dark object against a light background (the opposite was true of Rembrandt). The brushwork, like that of Rembrandt, is changeable, alternating between a thick concentration and light strokes. The painting shows Fabritius's interest in expressing daylight naturally and convincingly, a technique that was further refined by Vermeer.

HARMENSZ VAN RIJN REMBRANDT
(1606–69)

SELF-PORTRAIT WITH TURBAN

Gallery Sabauda, Turin. Celimage.sa/Scala Archives

REMBRANDT was born in Leiden, the son of a miller. He attended Leiden University for a while before abandoning his studies to become an artist's apprentice. In 1625, after six months studying in Amsterdam, Rembrandt returned to Leiden as an independent master. In about 1631 he settled in Amsterdam, where he was highly esteemed, especially for his portraits and historical group paintings. Rembrandt's wealth and happiness were short-lived: by the end of the 1640s his wife and three of his four children had died, and by 1658 he was bankrupt. These personal tragedies are reflected in his later work: the drama of his early paintings disappears as he focuses ever more on the emotional, rather than the physical, moments of his narratives.

In Rembrandt's lifetime the Baroque style was the favored mode of artistic expression. Unlike Rubens (1577–1640), Rembrandt did not adhere to the ideals of the Italian Renaissance, choosing instead to focus on the reality of the human condition. His work was expressive and emotionally literate, capturing the personality of his subjects and baring his emotions in numerous self-portraits such as this one.

PIETER DE HOOCH (1629–84)

WOMAN AND A MAID WITH A PAIL
IN A COURTYARD

Hermitage, St Petersburg. Celimage.sa/Scala Archives

BORN in Rotterdam, Pieter de Hooch moved to Delft in 1654, where he is recorded as both painter and manservant to a rich merchant. In Delft he came into contact with Fabritius (1622–54) and Nicolaes Maes (1632–93), both early members of the Delft School. De Hooch depicted scenes of middle-class domestic life, portraying Dutch ideals of domesticity. Jan Vermeer (1632–75) soon added to this genre and, with his greater skill, overshadowed him. By 1667 de Hooch had settled in Amsterdam, where he portrayed subjects from the upper classes, but his later paintings were less successful. He died in an insane asylum in 1684.

De Hooch's paintings have complex structures that create the illusion of real perspective. Rectangular architectural frames and blocks give the impression of distance and lead the viewer's eye to the main focus of the painting, such as the two women by the canal in *Woman and a Maid with a Pail*. The receding floor tiles help to create this impression of perspective.

As well as his mastery of perspective, de Hooch was skilled in the portrayal of natural light falling on a scene. His light is warm—more intense than Vermeer's—and his color range is richer, with fewer cool tones.

JAN VERMEER (1632–75)

THE MILKMAID

Rijksmuseum, Amsterdam. Celimage.sa/Lessing Archive

IT is believed that Jan Vermeer worked primarily as an art dealer. Little is known of his life and only around 35 paintings can definitely be attributed to him. He achieved little recognition for his own art and died in poverty at the age of 43, leaving a widow and 11 children. It was not until the 1860s and the resurgence of interest in artistic naturalism that Vermeer gained critical acclaim. He created his extremely realistic images using several techniques, including the camera obscura (based on the same principles as early photography).

Vermeer is best known for scenes of everyday domestic life, exemplified by such paintings as *The Milkmaid*. The painting shows us a moment frozen in time—there is a stillness, a lack of action that increases the feeling that we are peeping into the hidden, interior life of another person. The aura of calm that pervades many of Vermeer's paintings is generated by his predominant use of cool blues and yellows. He shows us the scene with a detached but somehow ennobling light, as if attempting to show us the dignity and poetry of the woman's life. The woman's pose and the superbly natural light coming through the window enhance this feeling.

MEINDERT HOBBEMA (1638–1709)

THE AVENUE AT MIDDELHARNIS

The National Gallery, London. Celimage.sa/Lessing Archive

HOBBEMA was a student of van Ruisdael during the late 1650s. He was a landscape painter of considerable skill, with an eye for detail that later made his paintings popular with English painters of the eighteenth and nineteenth centuries. In 1668 Hobbema married and became an excise officer in Amsterdam; his output declined thereafter.

While his work was indebted to that of van Ruisdael, Hobbema brought his own values and insights to the Dutch landscape genre. Hobbema's style is close to that of van Ruisdael but he veers away from the high drama of his master's works, instead painting peaceful, gentle scenes of an idyllic countryside. His use of light is integral to this difference in style—Hobbema's landscapes are sunnier, more expansive, and less oppressive. Van Ruisdael's sense of isolation is not found in Hobbema's work, which frequently includes figures, both human and animal.

Hobbema was faithful to the reality of the landscape and did not include fictional enhancements, which may explain his limited range; he is best known for his numerous paintings of mills. His most famous painting, *The Avenue at Middelharnis*, with elegant trees and a spacious, flat landscape, was especially appealing to the Baroque palette.

JEAN ANTOINE WATTEAU (1684–1721)

GILES AS PIERROT

Courtesy of the Ann Ronan Picture Library

WATTEAU was a key artist of the French Rococo style. In 1702 he moved to Paris, where he discovered an interest in theatrical costume and scenes. While working at the Luxembourg Palace, he admired a series of paintings by Rubens featuring the life of Marie de' Medici. These became the main influence on his style, but he also studied the Venetians, especially Veronese.

Watteau composed his paintings using drawings, often using the same ones over and over again. The drawings, in red, white, and black, and kept in a bound volume, have survived better than many of his paintings; Watteau lacked sophistication in the technical use of oils.

Watteau excelled as a painter of *fêtes galantes*—charming outdoor scenes—a title created for him in 1717 on his entry into the Academy, and took his subjects from the theater. Charming though they are, with a fairytale quality, his paintings often contain a note of melancholy despite the apparent gaiety. In this work, the clown figure appears lonely and forlorn.

WILLIAM HOGARTH (1697–1764)

MARIAGE À LA MODE

The National Gallery, London. Celimage.sa/Lessing Archive

HOGARTH trained as an engraver in the Rococo tradition and was an established engraver of bill-heads by 1720. He studied painting at the Academy in St Martin's Lane and by 1729 he was making a name for himself with his "conversation" pieces— small paintings showing polite social scenes. In 1730 he began to paint portraits, but although gifted, he did not have the flattering temperament of a successful portraitist.

Although he is remembered primarily as an engraver, Hogarth's painting was extremely skillful. He despised the effect of foreign influences on the English, making only occasional forays into painting in the fashionable Italian "Grand Manner." These are not considered his best works. This painting, one of the first in Hogarth's series of satirical scenes, was directed as much at the foibles of society as at its immorality. It portrays the setting of a contemporary play, *The Beggar's Opera*. It depicts a scene from the series on marriage in eighteenth-century England.

Other paintings in Hogarth's series of satirical works included melodramas such as *The Rake's Progress*, in which, as in *Mariage à la Mode*, there was a suitable punishment for the unscrupulous anti-heroes.

JEAN-BAPTISTE-SIMÉON CHARDIN (1699–1779)

HOUSE OF CARDS

Louvre, Paris. Celimage.sa/Lessing Archive

CHARDIN, a contemporary of Boucher (1703–70), was a painter in the popular bourgeois Dutch Realist style. He studied with portrait artist Noel-Nicolas Coypel (1628–1707) and worked on the Grande Galerie at the Palace of Fontainebleau.

As his style was popular and he worked slowly, Chardin often had to copy his paintings to please his buyers. In his last years, when he was ill, he began to use pastels. Using this faster medium, he produced three masterpieces—*Self-Portrait with Spectacles* (1771), *Self-Portrait with Eyeshade* (1771), and *Madame Chardin* (1775).

Chardin first exhibited his paintings in 1728, and became a member of the Academy in the same year. His still lifes are of food and kitchen utensils, but they have a depth beyond mere realism. His experiments with impasto and scumbled paint had an admirable depth of tone. By the early 1730s he began to paint unsentimental bourgeois genre scenes such as *House of Cards*, using warm but grayish colors. These were very successful when he exhibited them, and for a time he painted only small domestic scenes.

GIOVANNI ANTONIO CANALETTO (1697–1768)

SCENES FROM THE GRAND CANAL, VENICE

Pinacoteca di Brera, Milan. Celimage.sa/Scala Archives

INITIALLY Canaletto painted scenery for theaters with his father, but after a visit to Rome in 1719 he turned to painting pictures of views. By 1723, his handling of paint exhibited the luminosity and contrast of light and shade that made him famous.

English Consul Joseph Smith promoted Canaletto's work among British travelers to Venice, arranging exhibitions and encouraging the artist to extend his range to include views of Rome and *caprici*—pictures of real buildings set in imaginary scenes. Canaletto also painted pictures of Venice during the festivals and made a series of etchings and drawings, in pen, and pen and wash.

Canaletto made three trips to England, in 1746–50, 1752–53, and 1754–55, but they were not a success. He painted many views of London and country houses but his work became increasingly mannered. He returned to Venice and, although he worked until his death, much of his later painting is considered overly mechanical as he used a camera obscura to aid his composition.

This work has all the characteristics of Canaletto's later work, skillfully recording the effects of light and shade on the stonework and water. It depicts his favorite themes: the canals and their teeming life against a backdrop of detailed architecture.

GIOVANNI BATTISTA TIEPOLO (1696–1770)

AMERICA (DETAIL)

Episcopal Residence, Würzburg. Celimage.sa/Lessing Archive

A VENETIAN, Tiepolo was the greatest decorative Italian painter of the eighteenth century, and the purest of the Italian Rococo artists. He trained under historical painter Gregorio Lazzarini (1655–1730) but his studies of Veronese and contemporary painter Giovanni Battista Piazzetta (1683–1754) had a greater impact on his style.

In 1719 Tiepolo married Cecilia, sister of fellow artists the Guardi brothers. At the time of his marriage, his palette began to lighten and he left behind the dark, somber tones of Piazzetta and the seventeenth century. By 1725, when he had his first important commission—the fresco decorations at the archbishop's palace in Udine (finished in 1728)—his fresh handling, light tones, pale colors, and loose style were obvious.

Between 1741–50 Tiepolo was mainly active in Venice. In 1750 he was invited to Würzburg to decorate the Rococo bishop's palace. This figure, representing the continent of America, is part of the allegorical decoration Tiepolo executed here in collaboration with assistants and his sons Giandomenico and Lorenzo.

In 1755 Tiepolo was elected first President of the Venetian Academy and between 1762 and 1766 decorated the ceilings of the Royal Palace in Madrid. He died there suddenly in 1770 as the Rococo style was giving way to the Neoclassical movement.

JEAN-HONORÉ FRAGONARD (1732–1806)

THE PRIZE OF A KISS

Hermitage, St Petersburg. Celimage.sa/Scala Archives

BRIEFLY a pupil of Chardin in 1750, Fragonard studied with Boucher until 1752, when he won the Prix de Rome. He visited Rome in 1756, where he studied the works of Tiepolo. On his return to Paris, he made his name with a history painting in the "Grand Manner," *High Priest Coroesus Sacrificing Himself to Save Callirhoe* (1765). However, once accepted into the Academy, he gave up historical painting and turned to lighter subjects, such as *The Swing* (c.1766). Although such works often had erotic overtones, they managed to escape accusations of vulgarity through the artist's graceful and lighthearted handling of his subject matter. After his marriage in 1769, Fragonard also painted scenes of family groups.

He worked for the French court of Louis XVI, particularly for his beautiful mistress Mme du Barry. After the Revolution of 1789 and the Terror that followed, Fragonard's patrons disappeared. During this period he fled to Grasse in southern France, returning to Paris in poverty. He was found a job by the Neoclassical artist Jacques-Louis David (1748–1825) but died in obscurity.

This sketch, in keeping with the light-hearted Rococo subject matter, is painted with a light touch and spontaneity of movement. The colors are soft and bright and there is an element of cheekiness typical of Fragonard.

ANGELICA KAUFFMANN (1741–1807)

THE SELLER OF LOVES

Musée Lecoq, Clermont-Ferrand. Celimage.sa/Lessing Archive

THE daughter of Swiss painter Joseph John Kauffmann, Angelica Kauffmann was a child prodigy, executing commissions before the age of 13. She traveled with her father in Austria and Italy, where she copied the art of Correggio and Carracci.

In 1766, Kauffmann visited London and here, under the influence of Sir Joshua Reynolds (1723–92) and Benjamin West (1738–1820), her artistic style began to take on a Neoclassical flavor. Her portrait style reflected that of Reynolds, with whom there was talk of a clandestine affair. She produced decorative panels for the architect Robert Adam (1728–92) and, although her work is in the Neoclassical mould, there is a prettiness about it that suggests the Rococo.

Kauffmann made a disastrous first marriage to a bogus Italian count, but was remarried to decorative painter Antonio Zucchi (1726–95) in 1781, when she went to live in Rome. She produced many portraits and decorative paintings but preferred historical painting. Her clients included the royal courts of Naples, Russia, and Austria. Often dismissed as a decorative painter, she achieved financial success and was a founder member of the Royal Academy in London.

FRANÇOIS BOUCHER (1703–70)

VULCAIN PRESENTANT À VENUS DES ARMES POUR ÉNÉE

Louvre, Paris. Celimage.sa/Lessing Archive

BOUCHER was a leading exponent of Rococo decorative art, painting charming and often salacious mythological and pastoral scenes, although he also painted portraits, designs for tapestries, ceiling decorations, and accessories such as fans and shoes. His style was influenced by the works of Veronese, Rubens, and Watteau.

He began his career as an engraver of Watteau's works, winning the Prix de Rome in 1721. He traveled to Rome in 1727, returning to Paris in 1731, where he became a fashionable artist—his work epitomized the elegance and frivolity of court life. His most discerning patron was Madame de Pompadour, the mistress of Louis XVI. Boucher painted her several times and he also taught her to draw. He became the director of the Gobelins tapestry factory in 1755, Director of the Academy and King's Painter in 1765.

This subject was often treated by Boucher and the Louvre has three other versions. The design was originally for a series of tapestries, and is typically reflective of the spirit of Rococo tradition.

Rococo

HENRY FUSELI (1741–1825)

THE NIGHTMARE

Goethe Museum, Frankfurt. Courtesy of Edimedia

HENRY Fuseli was born in Switzerland, the son of a painter and writer, Johann Caspar Fuseli (sometimes spelt Füssli, 1707–82). His father's love of art and literature was transmitted to his son, manifesting itself in such works as *The Death of Oedipus* (1784) and *Titania and Bottom* (c.1780–90), as well as in Henry's later career as an art critic.

At the age of 20, Henry Fuseli was ordained as a pastor, but a disagreement with his father prompted him to leave Switzerland and the church. He traveled throughout Europe, studying in Germany and Italy, where he was influenced by Michelangelo (1475–1564), before arriving in London. He was soon accepted into the London art world and became a member of the Royal Academy in 1790. Despite frequent visits to Europe, including to his native Switzerland, he always returned to London.

Fuseli's enigmatic, dreamlike *Nightmare* was exhibited at the Royal Academy in 1790, bringing him wide public acclaim and instant fame. The unsettling subject matter and treatment reveal the disparate influences of Classicism (engendered by his study of Michelangelo), the grotesque, as seen in the work of Arcimboldo, and the work of William Blake (1757–1827).

GEORGE STUBBS (1724–1806)

MARES AND FOALS

Private Collection. Celimage.sa/Lessing Archive

GEORGE Stubbs was born in Liverpool in 1724. Although his art education was informal and short, he showed a flair for portraiture. He used this skill to support himself during time spent studying anatomy in York. In 1756, on his return to England after traveling in Italy, George Stubbs led an isolated existence while he devoted himself to further anatomical study, which was now exclusively of horses. Stubbs moved to London in 1760, where his lifelike paintings of sporting and racing events found a large audience. The year 1766 saw the publication of his *Anatomy of the Horse*. He died leaving a further, unpublished, text on the comparative anatomy of humans, tigers, and common fowl.

Stubbs's accomplished paintings of horses brought him many aristocratic patrons. His skill at depicting a horse's form came from his carefully gained anatomical knowledge. For each painting, Stubbs made in-depth studies of musculature and movement before beginning to work. Stubbs's paintings reveal a high level of "finish" as well as painstaking attention to detail.

Although Stubbs is remembered now for his reverential paintings of horses, he also produced paintings of various other animals, as well as portraits and conversation pieces.

Romantic

WILLIAM BLAKE (1757–1827)

ISAAC NEWTON

Tate Gallery, London. Celimage.sa/Lessing Archive

WILLIAM Blake was born in London. His figure drawing was learned by copying plaster casts of ancient statues under the tutelage of Henry Pars (c.1733–1806). He trained briefly at London's Royal Academy, although he did not agree with the principles of the school or the teachings of Sir Joshua Reynolds. He still continued to exhibit at the Academy throughout his life.

Blake was a visionary, a poet and artist who strove for social and political freedom for all. His works ranged from the religious, such as *The Ancient of Days*, to the grotesque, such as *Ghost of a Flea* (1819–20). Along with his contemporary, the Spanish painter and etcher Goya (1746–1828), Blake rebelled against the accepted teachings of the contemporary art world, disrupting eighteenth-century art with his terrifying emotions and radical perspectives. Blake's writings included two collections of poems called *Songs of Innocence* (1789) and *Songs of Experience* (1794), and the famous hymn "Jerusalem." At his death he was part way through illustrating the works of Dante Alighieri (1265–1321).

Sir Isaac Newton (1642–1727) was Britain's most accomplished mathematician, scientist, and philosopher. Here Blake creates a stark portrait of the genius at work. To Blake, Newton represented the elevation of reason; he was the mythic author of the mechanistic universe.

JOHN MARTIN (1789–1854)

THE GREAT DAY OF HIS WRATH

Tate Gallery, London. Courtesy of Edimedia

WITH the emergence of the Romantic movement in the eighteenth century, art turned toward the splendor of nature and man's spiritual relationship with it. John Martin was one of the major exponents of Romantic painting. Born in Northumberland, he began his career as an enamel painter. Martin's volume of work is relatively small—his career was cut short when he suffered a stroke. He painted several biblical stories but, rather than focusing on the human narrative, he chose to show stormy, dramatic landscapes that evoke intensely turbulent emotions. In common with other Romantic painters, Martin took inspiration from the literary works of poets Lord Byron (1788–1824) and John Milton (1608–74), as well as from Nordic myths. He did not paint realistic landscapes. His painting sprang from an internal vision, earning him the nickname "Mad Martin."

Many of his paintings have an overwhelming physical presence. He used large canvases, filling them with passionate scenes that intimidated the viewer. *The Great Day of his Wrath*, as do many of his works, includes tiny figures set in the foreground against a domineering landscape. This technique emphasizes the insignificance of man when compared to the solidity of nature, as personified by the aggressive nature of the sky.

FRANCISCO GOYA Y LUCIENTES (1746–1828)

EXECUTION OF THE DEFENDERS OF MADRID, MAY 3RD, 1808

Prado, Madrid. Celimage.sa/Lessing Archive

SPANISH painter Goya spent his early career in Saragossa and moved to Madrid in 1763. Here he was trained by Francisco Bayeu y Subías (1734–95), whose sister he married in 1773. Between 1775 and 1792 he designed tapestries in the Rococo style and painted portraits and religious scenes.

In 1792, Goya suffered an unknown illness that left him deaf. He became introspective and obsessed with the morbid and bizarre themes that haunted his later work. He also found fame with his portraits, becoming court painter to Charles IV in 1799.

In 1808 Spain was invaded by France and Joseph Bonaparte was placed on the Spanish throne. Goya was sickened by the barbarity of the French soldiers, executing this painting in response to a bloody incident in May 1808 when their troops murdered Spanish civilians. This is one of his most forceful and emotive works—the pathos of the condemned man's gesture, illuminated in a white shirt by the lantern light, is intensely moving.

In 1820, he painted 14 murals, known as his "Black Paintings," showing dark, horrific scenes that were painted in a free, almost Impressionistic manner. In 1824 he was exiled to France, where he was employed as a portrait painter by the French royal family.

SIR THOMAS LAWRENCE (1769–1830)

THE CHILDREN OF JOHN ANGERSTEIN, JOHN JULIUS WILLIAM (1801–1866), CAROLINE AMELIA (DIED 1879), ELIZABETH JULIA, AND HENRY FREDERIC (1805–1821)

Louvre, Paris. Celimage.sa/Lessing Archive

ENGLISH portrait painter Sir Thomas Lawrence was one of the most talented artists of his time. Almost entirely self-taught, he studied at the Royal Academy in London in 1786–87, and was accepted as an Academician in 1791. His first full-length portrait, *Lady Cremone* (1789), led to his portrait of Queen Charlotte, which he exhibited in 1791 to great acclaim. He succeeded Sir Joshua Reynolds in 1792 as painter to King George III.

By 1806 Lawrence had consolidated his talent, and half-length portraits of men replaced the stylish full-length female portraits of his earlier period. He was knighted in 1815 and sent to Europe as an envoy of the Prince Regent (the future George IV) in 1818 to paint the heads of state and military leaders who had been involved in the defeat of Napoleon. He visited Venice and Rome in 1818, where he painted Pope Pius VII. His portrait style emulated that of Reynolds, but had a fashionable note of modernity and theatricality—he often lowered the horizon, for example, as in this painting, to silhouette his figures sharply against the sky.

THÉODORE GÉRICAULT (1791–1824)

THE DRESSAGE

Louvre, Paris. Courtesy of the Ann Ronan Picture Library

GÉRICAULT'S career lasted for only a decade; for someone with such a small body of work, he had a huge impact. He studied in Paris with both Carle Vernet (1758–1836) and Pierre Guérin (1774–1833), but he was influenced more by the Old Masters, especially Rubens (1577–1640). His subject matter—horses and contemporary subjects—shows the influence of Antoine-Jean Gros (1771–1835), Napoleon's official war painter.

Géricault visited Italy in 1816–18, and on his return to Paris he exhibited *The Raft of the Medusa* (1819). Although it received the gold medal at the Salon, it still caused a political scandal because its subject matter appeared to imply criticism of the government. The epic treatment of a contemporary event was also innovative.

Between 1820 and 1822 Géricault visited England, during which time he painted jockeys and racecourses and made lithographs showing the poverty that was rife on the streets of London. From 1822 to 1823 he painted ten portraits of patients at La Salpetrière, the lunatic asylum in Paris. The spontaneous brushwork of *The Dressage* and the drama of the pose and lighting are typical of Géricault's Romantic style. The influence on the young contemporary artist Delacroix (1798–1863) is easy to see.

Géricault died tragically early after falling from a horse.

Romantic

124

JOHN CONSTABLE (1776–1837)

LIFE-SIZE STUDY FOR THE HAYWAIN

Victoria and Albert Museum, London. Celimage.sa/Scala Archives

CONSTABLE was born in Suffolk, the son of a wealthy industrialist; he lived there until 1795, when he moved to London. Although he received some early training, Constable was largely self-taught until 1799, when he entered the Royal Academy. The countryside was to remain an inspiration to him throughout his life—he was fascinated by the effects of light and by cloud formations.

Although he was influenced by Claude Lorrain (1600–82) and Poussin (1594–1665), Constable preferred to learn his art from nature, rather than from other artists' interpretations of it. He was averse to studio work, preferring to paint out of doors.

In middle age Constable suffered from severe depression, and this is reflected in the brooding light, dark, lowering clouds, and gloomy atmosphere of many of his later works, such as *The Valley Farm* (1835) and *Stoke-by-Nayland* (1836–37). Here, the brushwork is less distinct—almost Impressionistic— in contrast with the clarity of his earlier paintings, such as *The Haywain*.

The Haywain was painted on a visit to his native Stour Valley, an area to which he often returned. The colors of the sky, the wate,r and the dappled light on the field are indicative of the many hours Constable spent sketching nature to perfect his technique.

Romantic

EUGÈNE DELACROIX (1798–1863)

MASSACRE AT CHIOS

Louvre, Paris. Celimage.sa/Scala Archives

DELACROIX began his career as a musician, and his decision to become an artist was aided by his friend and teacher Géricault (1791–1824). It may be no coincidence that this emotive picture was painted in the year of Géricault's death. Alongside Géricault, Delacroix became a leading figure of the nineteenth-century Romantic movement in French art. There was a constant rivalry between Delacroix and the other, more conventional leading painter of the day, Ingres (1780–1867). Delacroix traveled to England in 1825, where he greatly admired the work of English painter John Constable (1776–1837).

Massacre at Chios relates an incident from the Greco-Turkish War in 1824. As the Greeks struggled to liberate themselves from Turkish occupation, over 20,000 soldiers were slaughtered by their oppressors. In the painting, Delacroix emphasizes the Turk's brutality by his impassivity; his face looks down, without emotion, at the carnage beneath him. Delacroix was sympathetic to the Greeks' cause, but his journal records that he chose the subject matter for its topicality, assuring maximum publicity for his work.

CASPAR DAVID FRIEDRICH (1774–1840)

NORTHERN SEA BY MOONLIGHT

Narodni Galerie, Prague. Celimage.sa/Lessing Archive

CASPAR David Friedrich was one of the foremost German Romantic landscape painters. He attended Copenhagen Academy from 1794 to 1798 but was largely self-taught. He moved to Dresden in 1798, where he moved in Romantic literary circles, and remained there for most of his life.

Initially he was a topographical artist, working in pencil and wash. He took up oil painting in 1807, and his first commission, *Cross on the Mountain* (1808), an altarpiece for a private chapel, caused controversy because the spirituality of his landscape was considered sacrilegious.

His introspective and melancholic subjects, which included cemeteries in the snow, fog-bound landscapes, and seashores at dusk, were often ground-breaking. He suffered a stroke in 1835 and thereafter returned to working in sepia. His work was virtually forgotten until its rediscovery by artists of the Symbolist movement.

Northern Sea by Moonlight is a carefully crafted painting depicting a desolate coastal scene at dusk. The painting, despite its somber palette, is rich and evocative in its depiction of a deserted shoreline.

Romantic

THOMAS COLE (1801–48)

THE CROSS IN THE WILDERNESS OR
THE LONELY CROSS—AFTER A POEM BY
FELICIA HAYMANS

Musée d'Orsay, Paris. Celimage.sa/Lessing Archive

COLE lived in England until the age of 17, when his family, who were part American, part English, moved to Ohio in America. He had begun his artistic training in England and was able to continue his studies at the Philadelphia Academy of Art. In later years he helped found and was considered the leader of the Hudson River School, a group of artists who shared a love of the emptiness and monumentality of the American landscape and strove to capture its grandeur on canvas. They worked mainly around the Hudson River and the nearby Catskill Mountains and paid great attention to the showing of nature in its overwhelming detail. Cole was also instrumental in establishing the Romantic movement within the American art world.

The Cross in the Wilderness or The Lonely Cross typifies the ethereal, almost heavenly landscapes depicted by the Hudson River school. The soft evening light casts shadows across the scene and a girl sits deep in thought under the setting sun. Fall colors touch the treetops as the distance recedes to a far and distant horizon.

WILLIAM ETTY (1787–1849)

BACCHANTE WITH TAMBOURINE

Louvre, Paris. Celimage.sa/Lessing Archive

WILLIAM Etty was one of the few British painters to paint nudes, for which he was viewed with suspicion. He was born in York but studied in London, training at the Royal Academy and then with Sir Thomas Lawrence (1769–1830), whose influence intially included a warm use of color that was later modified by Etty's trips to Italy.

He visited Europe several times and studied artists such as Pierre-Narcisse Guérin (1774–1833), Titian, and van Dyck—all highly skilled colorists. He met French Romantic painter Delacroix in 1828. The work of Rubens was influential in creating the sensual, glowing style that Etty primarily applied to his nude female studies; as a result, his work was often considered lush and indecent.

Etty's paintings show faithful studies of nudes, presented as mythological or historical characters. He studied life drawing at the Royal Academy throughout his life. His drawings are now his most admired works—many of his paintings seem vapid by comparison. He lived in poverty, achieving fame only shortly before his death.

JOSEPH MALLORD WILLIAM TURNER
(1775–1851)

ULYSSES DERIDING POLYPHEMUS

Tate Gallery, London. Celimage.sa/Lessing Archive

A KEY figure of the Romantic movement, Turner is also popularly viewed as the greatest English landscape painter. Born in London, the son of a baker, Turner refused to hide his humble background and retained both his Cockney accent and manners, despite his aristocratic friends and patronage. He received his initial training from an architectural topographer before entering the Royal Academy in 1789, where he exhibited at the age of 15. In 1791 he toured North Wales and Scotland before traveling to Switzerland, making sketches and watercolors of landscapes. Turner's main subjects were land or seascapes and historical narratives. By the middle of his career he focused on an emotive, instinctual representation of light and the drama of extreme weather. The accurate portrayal in painting of the effect of light at different times of day became more important to him than recording a representation of the true facts. Turner's late paintings are blurred, with whirls of seeping colors. In this respect they anticipate the loose brushwork of the Impressionist movement.

In this painting Ulysses has just escaped from the giant, Polyphemus, whom he has blinded. Ulysses flees with his companions, while the giant throws rocks at their ship from the top of the mountain. Ulysses taunts him with a torch from the prow of the vessel. Nereids, with stars on their foreheads, swim playfully around the ship.

PAUL DELAROCHE (1797–1856)

THE CHILDREN OF EDWARD IV IN THE TOWER

Louvre, Paris. Celimage.sa/Lessing Archive

ALTHOUGH his uncle, Adrien-Jacques Joly, offered him a post in the Bibliothèque Nationale, Delaroche was set upon becoming artist. As his brother Jules-Hippolyte was then studying history painting with Jaques Louis David, his father decided that Paul should take up landscape painting, and in 1816 he entered the Ecole des Beaux-Arts.

Delaroche made his début at the Paris Salon in 1822 with *Christ Descended from the Cross* (1822) and *Jehosheba Saving Joash* (1822). The latter work clearly showed the influence of Gros, and it was greatly praised by Géricault. At the same Salon, Delacroix exhibited *Dante and Virgil in Hell* (1822), a highly influential painting, which could be said to mark the arrival of Romanticism in Paris, with its challenge to the dominance of Neo-classicism. Delaroche's response to this conflict of influences was to steer a course between the two currents, unwilling to adopt Romanticism for fear of jeopardizing his public standing. Such a compromise can be seen in his entry for the Salon of 1824, *Joan of Arc in Prison* (1824), and it was the distinguishing feature of his subsequent works.

Delaroche was famous for his portraits and sentimental historical scenes, such as *The Children of Edward IV in the Tower*. The boys, Edward V and Richard, were allegedly murdered by their uncle, King Richard III.

CURRIER (1813–88) AND IVES (1824–95)

PRAIRIE FIRES OF THE GREAT WEST

Courtesy of the Ann Ronan Picture Library

FROM 1834 to 1907 the lithography shop of Currier & Ives produced in excess of a million prints, which included more than 7,500 titles.

Lithography involves grinding a piece of limestone flat and smooth, and then drawing in a mirror image on the stone with a special grease pencil. After the image is completed, the stone is etched with a solution of aqua fortis, a chemical, leaving the greased areas in slight relief. Water is then used to wet the stone and greased-ink is rolled on to the raised areas. Since grease and water do not mix, the greased-ink is repelled by the moisture on the stone and clings to the original grease pencil lines. The stone is then placed in a press and used as a printing block to imprint black and white images on paper.

Prairie Fires of the Great West depicts a train with cowcatcher and headlamp crossing the prairie. Frightened buffalo stampede in the face of the fire that is blazing across the prairie, producing billows of dark, acrid-looking smoke. There is an impression of speed and urgency in the face of the great danger posed by the conflagration.

SIR EDWIN LANDSEER (1802–73)

FIGHTING DOGS PAUSING FOR BREATH

Louvre, Paris. Celimage.sa/Lessing Archive

EDWIN Landseer was a successful English painter, sculptor, and engraver who specialized in the depiction of animals. The son of John Landseer, an engraver and writer, Edwin was an infant prodigy, exhibiting at the Royal Academy aged 12, and becoming an Academician at 24. He refused the presidency in 1865.

The excellent draftsmanship and fluid technique of Landseer's early career gave way to sentimental genre scenes of animal, which were meant to imply the natural morality of the animal kingdom. These mawkish images were highly prized in Victorian England and became widely available as engravings, many executed by Landseer's brother, Thomas (1798–1880). Landseer led a socially and professionally successful life, and was a favorite of Queen Victoria and was friendly with the novelists Charles Dickens (1812–70) and William Thackeray (1811–63). He visited Scotland regularly, producing such well known works as *Monarch of the Glen*. Hunting scenes and landscapes were popular subjects for English school painters for most of the nineteenth century.

Tragically, Landseer became mentally ill in 1869 and died four years later. He is buried in London's St Paul's Cathedral.

Romantic

THOMAS GAINSBOROUGH (1727–88)

CONVERSATION IN THE PARK

Louvre, Paris. Celimage.sa/Scala Archives

GAINSBOROUGH was born in Sudbury, Suffolk. He was, at heart, a landscape painter, although he painted portraits for a living. He went to London in around 1740, where he studied as an engraver with Hubert-François Gravelot (1699–1773), who had been a pupil of Antoine Watteau. In 1759 he moved to Bath and painted society portraits, developing an elegant, glamorous style inspired by van Dyck. He was noted for his exact likenesses, something his rival Sir Joshua Reynolds (1723–92) found detrimental to the grandeur of his own paintings.

In 1768 Gainsborough was elected to the Royal Academy in London and four years later he moved to the capital. His style developed into light brushstrokes and delicate colors. From the 1780s he painted genre pictures of peasants in a style after Murillo (1618–82), as an extension of his interest in landscape. He painted and drew landscapes throughout his life.

Conversation in the Park is very traditionalist and notably innocent in comparison with Gainsborough's later works. The couple are positioned in such a way that we can still see the surrounding landscape.

JOHANN ZOFFANY (1733–1810)

CHARLES TOWNELEY'S LIBRARY IN PARK STREET

Towneley Hall Art Gallery and Museum, Burnley. Celimage.sa/Lessing Archive

JOHANN Zoffany was born and educated in Germany. Like many artists before him, he traveled to Italy to study the Classical and Renaissance masters. In Rome, Zoffany studied under fellow German Anton Mengs (1728–79). By 1760 Zoffany had moved to London, where he became one of the founding members of the Royal Academy. His client list soon included included King George III and other members of the royal family. As well as society portraits Zoffany produced theater decorations and several "conversation pieces," group portraits that show the sitters occupied in an activity. Several of his conversation pieces depict groups of cultured men surrounded by art, and *Charles Towneley's Library in Park Street* is a good example.

Here, Towneley is seen in profile, with his dog by his feet. The room is filled with Classical sculptures, friezes, and busts. The men in the group are shown studying books or conversing. Zoffany succeeds in portraying the men as the intellectual, rational leaders of their society, while at the same time showing off their excellent taste and obvious wealth.

JACQUES-LOUIS DAVID (1748–1825)

DEATH OF MARAT

Royal Beaux-Arts Museum of Belgium, Brussels. Celimage.sa/Lessing Archive

JACQUES-LOUIS David was a leading figure in the French Revolution, as well as the foremost French Neoclassical painter. A student of Boucher (1703–70) and the teacher of Ingres (1780–1867), David became an integral part of the French art establishment.

David was a fervent supporter of Napoleon (1769–1821), whom he depicted on several canvases, and was among the influential citizens of France who passed judgment on Louis XVI. Jean-Paul Marat was a leader of the French Revolution of 1789, and a friend of David. Marat became a martyr to the cause when he was stabbed to death in his bath by Charlotte Corday, a fervent royalist. The letter he holds in his hand was her faked letter of introduction, with which she had fraudulently entered his home.

Death of Marat was a personal homage to a friend, as seen by the inscription on the side of the makeshift desk, as well as a historical record. The portrayal, particularly fine in the brushwork recreating the corpse, is a technique that can be seen in the work of Ingres.

SIR HENRY RAEBURN (1756–1823)

INNOCENCE, PORTRAIT OF NANCY GRAHAM

Louvre, Paris. Celimage.sa/Lessing Archive

HENRY Raeburn was born near Edinburgh and began his career painting miniatures, a skill that he taught himself. In about 1776 Raeburn switched to painting portraits and became the leading Scottish portrait painter of his generation. Following his advantageous marriage in 1778, Raeburn became financially secure, enabling him to travel. In 1785, after visiting Sir Joshua Reynolds (1723–1792) in London, he traveled to Italy where he studied in Rome for several years. However, the years spent abroad did not have a profound effect on Raeburn's style.

Returning in 1787, Raeburn settled in Edinburgh, and very quickly became a highly prolific portrait artist. It is estimated that Raeburn produced about one thousand portraits of the key people in Scottish society. In 1792 an exhibition of works by Raeburn was held in the Royal Academy, and in 1815 he was elected as a Royal Academician.

Innocence, Portrait of Nancy Graham is a delightful Georgian-style depiction of a young girl. A neutral backdrop enhances the charming naivety of her expression.

Neoclassical

SIR JOSHUA REYNOLDS (1723-92)

LOUIS-PHILIPPE JOSEPH D'ORLÉANS, DUC DE CHARTRES (PHILIPPE ÉGALITÉ)

Musée Condé, Chantilly. Celimage.sa/Lessing Archive

DURING his lifetime, Sir Joshua Reynolds was considered the finest portrait painter in England. Born in Plympton, Devon, he was apprenticed to Thomas Hudson (1701–79) and had his own workshop by the age of 20. In 1749 his former master sponsored a trip to Italy, where he studied Classical sculpture and the Renaissance masters. He assiduously copied the style of painting of the Renaissance masters, emulating their brushwork and using similar poses and iconography, in an attempt to simulate their grandeur. Reynolds' importance in art history is underlined by his academic achievements. He was the first president of the Royal Academy, which opened in 1768. He delivered 15 discourses on art to students there, and his opinions were respected by several generations of artists.

Reynolds' portrait of *Louis-Philippe Joseph d'Orléans* depicts the father of King Louis Philippe. He had voted for the death of Louis XVI, but he himself would ultimately be executed by the guillotine. This strikingly formal portrait lacks the warmth of other works by Reynolds.

JEAN-AUGUSTE-DOMINIQUE INGRES
(1780–1867)

THE BATHER

Louvre, Paris. Celimage.sa/Scala Archives

INGRES was sent to the Toulouse Academy at the age of 11 by his artist father. From there he went to Paris in 1797 to study with Jacques-Louis David (1748–1825). In 1801 he won the Prix de Rome, and went there in 1807. He stayed for 18 years, receiving little acclaim in Paris.

Ingres earned his living by painting and drawing portraits, although he also produced historical paintings. He was a skilled draftsman, noted for his sinuous line and expressive contour. However, although technically without reproach, he often distorted shapes, elongating them in the manner of Botticelli and Raphael. *La Grande Odalisque* (1814), one of several nudes painted in Rome, was criticized for having such a long back.

When Ingres returned to Paris in 1824, he became a leading figure of French Neoclassicism. Following his success, he spent much of his time working on two large works, including *The Apotheosis of Homer*, a ceiling painting for the Louvre, which was installed in 1827.

The superb draftsmanship and clarity of shapes, light, and line in *The Bather* are typical of Ingres's graceful nudes. Such works had a strong influence on Degas, whose many nude studies echo the scene shown here.

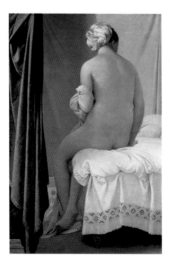

ANTONIO CANOVA (1757–1822)

THE THREE GRACES

Gipsoteca Canoviana, Possagno. Celimage.sa/Scala Archives

ANTONIO Canova was arguably the greatest sculptor of his time. His ability to turn marble into a likeness of living, supple flesh remains breathtaking to this day. In his own time his influence was such that, almost single-handedly, he turned the accepted fashion in sculpture from Baroque to Neoclassical. His ability to recreate the female form with sensuous accuracy is evident in *A Sleeping Nymph* (1820–22).

The son of a stonemason, Canova was born in Possagno, Italy, and worked as a sculptor from childhood. He left home at the age of 13, accompanying his sculpting master to Venice; he remained there until 1781, when he moved to Rome. Here, he became a great favorite of society, and of the Pope, who bestowed upon him the title Marchese d'Ischia. He had earned the honor by traveling to France to reclaim Italian works of art stolen by Napoleon's troops—he so impressed Napoleon by his courage that the leader attempted to persuade Canova to stay.

The Three Graces, admired for its purity of line and anatomical clarity, is one of Canova's best-known works. The sensuous curves and Canova's striving for symmetry in the design can be divined in this ensemble, and is also clearly evident in his masterful *Cupid and Psyche* (1793).

SIR JOHN EVERETT MILLAIS (1829–96)

OPHELIA

Tate Gallery, London. Celimage.sa/Lessing Archive

JOHN Everett Millais was born in Jersey. Recognizing his prodigious artistic talent, his parents moved to London to allow him to study at the Royal Academy. He was a universal favorite with both tutors and students, although his association with the Pre-Raphaelite Brotherhood (of which he was a founder member) caused the senior Academicians great alarm.

Early works, such as the exquisite *Lorenzo and Isabella* (1849) and his powerful portrait of John Ruskin (1853), prove the magnificence of Millais's artistic ability. In 1852 he exhibited *The Huguenot*, the overwhelming success of which projected him to the forefront of society at a time when the Pre-Raphaelite Brotherhood was in demise. He began painting much-coveted society portraits, as well as sentimental scenes that would appeal to Victorian art buyers.

Ophelia successfully portrays the Pre-Raphaelite fascination with legend, myth, and literature. Here, the tragic young woman floats in death alongside lush riverbank foliage.

Pre-Raphaelite

WILLIAM HOLMAN HUNT (1827–1910)

SELF-PORTRAIT

Uffizi Gallery, Florence. Celimage.sa/Scala Archives

WILLIAM Holman Hunt was a forceful member of the Pre-Raphaelite Brotherhood. An early mentor of Rossetti (1828–82), Hunt later quarrelled with his former friend about personal and professional matters—Rossetti had an affair with Hunt's first fiancée, and both men claimed to have been the guiding force behind the Pre-Raphaelite Brotherhood. Hunt was a great admirer of John Ruskin (1819–1900), and the only one of the seven members of the Pre-Raphaelite Brotherhood to adhere to its principles throughout his career—he chose religious and literary themes for his works and was a strong exponent of painting in natural light, rather than executing his work in the studio. When creating *The Light of the World* (1853) he spent several months painting by moonlight in his garden, earning himself a reputation locally as a madman. Hunt spent much of his life traveling, particularly in Europe and the Middle East, where he was inspired by the vibrant colors and clear light, as well as the local materials and architecture.

SIR EDWARD COLEY BURNE-JONES (1833–98)

KING COPHETUA AND THE BEGGAR MAID

Tate Gallery, London. Celimage.sa/Lessing Archive

BURNE-JONES and William Morris (1834–96), although not members of the Pre-Raphaelite movement, were extremely important to it. They are generally considered as the second generation of Pre-Raphaelites. Burne-Jones was a pupil of Rossetti (1828–82) and remained in awe of the older artist throughout his life. Much of his early work is almost indistinguishable from that of his teacher. However, by the end of his life, his work was defined entirely by his own individual style. His later work moved toward the burgeoning Art Nouveau movement. In common with other Pre-Raphaelites, Burne-Jones took much of his inspiration from literature, mythology, and legend.

This painting, from Burne-Jones's first *Pygmalion* series (1867–69), is based upon an old legend of a king who found that his love for a beggar maid was greater than all his wealth and power. The setting is influenced by the art of fifteenth-century Italy, particularly the work of Mantegna. The subject could be viewed as the elevation of love above everything else.

Pre-Raphaelite

THE BELOVED

Tate Gallery, London. Celimage.sa/Lessing Archive

DANTE Gabriel Rossetti, born in London of Italian parents, studied under Ford Madox Brown (1821–93) before sharing a studio with William Holman Hunt (1827–1910). In 1848, the two friends and Sir John Everett Millais (1829–96) set up the Pre-Raphaelite Brotherhood. All three artists became famous in their own right. Millais eventually turned to society portraits and works of crowd-pleasing sentimentality, while Hunt maintained his adherence to religious and spiritual subjects. However, Rossetti's work became more sensual, much of it portraying voluptuous women. The only ornamentation is in his rich palette and the opulent materials and jewels draping his models. Most of his models were also his lovers, including Elizabeth Siddal (1829–62), whom he married after a ten-year relationship, shortly before her tragic death.

Here, Rossetti uses the motif of roses both to organize the portraits and to ornament the work. The picture is based on a verse from the biblical "Song of Solomon," which describes a bride being brought forth by maidens, dressed in rich attire. The theme of love and marriage is suggested by the vase of roses in the foreground, which also provides the key to the composition. The face of the bride forms the central circle of a rose shape; around her the faces of her servants are arranged in an overlapping pattern, like the petals of a rose. The veils around the women's heads, which seem to form another layer of petals, enhance the floral shape, and the motif is repeated in the details of the work.

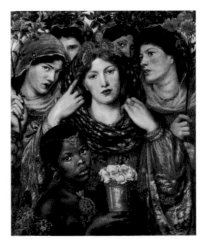

FORD MADOX BROWN (1821–1893)

THE SEEDS AND FRUITS OF ENGLISH POETRY

Ashmolean Museum, Oxford. Celimage.sa/Scala

BORN in Calais in 1821, Ford Madox Brown studied art in Antwerp and Paris. His contemporaries largely ignored his work, so he never made a great deal of money from the sale of his pictures. After a visit to Rome in 1845, he fell under the influence of the Nazarene School of painting, as expounded by the German painters Johann Overbeck (1789–1869) and Peter von Cornelius (1783–1867).

Madox Brown's subjects were often drawn from English literature and painted in a dark and dramatic style. He was almost incapable of finishing his paintings and was often unable to leave a work alone. Even when it was apparently finished, he would continually retouch it.

Although he was not a memeber of the pre-Raphaelite Brotherhood, in later years Madox Brown was regarded as the epitome of Pre-Raphaelite art. *The Seeds and Fruits of English Poetry* is a decidedly Pre-Raphaelite work, with its brilliant colors set in a sumptuous frame. At the center, we see Chaucer reading his "Legend of Custance" to Edward III and his court, assembled around the fountain of wisdom. Dante Gabriel Rosetti is the model for Chaucer. In the wings are Milton, Spenser, and Shakespeare. On the left are Byron, Pope, and Burns, and on the right are Goldsmith and Thomson, in the roundels; the names of Campbell, Moore, Shelley, Keats, Chatterton, Kirke White, Coleridge, and Wordsworth are written on the cartouches held by the standing children.

WILLIAM MORRIS (1834–96)

STRAWBERRY THIEF

Victoria and Albert Museum, London. Courtesy of the Ann Ronan Picture Library

WILLIAM Morris was a painter, designer, businessman, novelist, poet, and political activist. While at Oxford University he met Edward Burne-Jones (1833–98), with whom he struck up a lifelong friendship and artistic partnership. Morris was born into a wealthy family; he used his legacy to set up the business Morris and Co., for which Burne-Jones and Rossetti (1828–82), among others, provided designs. The firm produced textiles, tiles, furniture, and stained glass.

Strawberry Thief was one of the textile designs that Morris himself produced for the company. Many of his designs feature flowers or birds, an indication not only of his love of nature but also of the influence of aestheticism on his work.

As well as running a successful business, Morris published poetry and a utopian novel, *News from Nowhere*. He was a fervent socialist.

JOHN WILLIAM WATERHOUSE (1849–1917)

OPHELIA

Christie's Images, London. Courtesy of the Bridgeman Art Library

JOHN William Waterhouse was born in Italy, to English parents. He began his career as a painter in the Pre-Raphaelite mould, but went on to create his own style, perhaps best defined as Romantic Classicism. Waterhouse's conscious decision to ally himself with the Pre-Raphaelites can be seen in his duplication of their subjects, such as *Ophelia* and *The Lady of Shalott* (1888), and in his adherence to the teachings contained in Ruskin's *Modern Painters* (1843)—a book from which the Pre-Raphaelites drew inspiration. However, Waterhouse also looked to ancient cultures for material and was influenced by the art of Alma-Tadema (1836–1912) and Lord Leighton (1830–96). Toward the end of his life, his style was to some degree influenced by Impressionism.

Waterhouse's paintings are exquisitely detailed and executed with faithful attention to the subject's source, whether historical, mythological, or literary. In this painting, Waterhouse depicts the final moments of Ophelia's life, in contrast to Millais's famous *Ophelia* (1852), in which she has already drowned. Waterhouse balances Ophelia's virginal paleness by the use of funereal background colors.

Pre-Raphaelite

GUSTAVE COURBET (1819–77)

BONJOUR MONSIEUR COURBET

Fabre Museum, Montpellier. Celimage.sa/Lessing Archive

COURBET was born in Ornans, France. His art was largely self-taught, achieved by studying sixteenth- and seventeenth-century art—in particular the work of Caravaggio (1571–1610) and Rembrandt (1606–69). Courbet was at the forefront of artistic and political activism in nineteenth-century France. In 1873, following a spell in prison as a result of his political activities and inability to pay his debts, Courbet fled to Switzerland. He remained in exile until his death four years later.

In 1855, dissatisfied with the Paris Salon, Courbet staged an independent exhibition of his works. His political beliefs are evident in the self-portrait included in *Bonjour Monsieur Courbet*, notably in the defiant tilt of his chin and the firm grip on his stick. Courbet depicts himself (the figure striding on the right) as he is met by his patron, Alfred Bruyas.

The painting (also called *Le Rencontre*) demonstrates why Courbet was hailed as the premier Realist of his day: every detail, such as the braiding on Bruyas's jacket and the buttons on Courbet's walking boots, is minutely finished. Of the three figures, Courbet's self-portrait commands most attention as he moves toward the center of the canvas. The eyes of Bruyas and his dog, as well as those of the viewer, are all drawn toward Courbet.

JEAN FRANÇOIS MILLET (1814–75)

THE GLEANERS

Musée d'Orsay, Paris. Celimage.sa/Scala Archives

JEAN François Millet was born in Normandy, France, the son of a farm laborer. He studied locally with Bon du Mouchel (1807–46), from whom he learned his portrait skills. In 1837 he won a scholarship and moved to Paris to study under the historical painter Paul Delaroche (1797–1856), who passed on his skills to the young Millet.

In 1840 Millet set up his own studio, making a living as a portrait painter. In 1848 he had an overwhelming success with *The Winnower*, which he had exhibited at the Paris Salon. At about the same time he became involved with the Barbizon School, a group of landscape artists led by Théodore Rousseau (1812–67). He moved to Barbizon in 1849 but was never a member of the school, preferring to make people the focus of his landscapes, as in *The Gleaners*. Millet painted many pictures depicting the grim reality of French peasants toiling on the land, seen also in *The Sower* (c.1850) and *The Angelus* (1857–59), among others. The golden light of *The Gleaners* throws the peasant women in the foreground of the painting into sharp relief, heightening the sense of pathos. Millet used his paintings to reveal the harshness of poverty and social injustice; as a result he was considered to be a champion of left-wing political groups.

Realist

HONORÉ DAUMIER (1808–79)

THE LAUNDRESS

Musée d'Orsay, Paris. Celimage.sa/Lessing Archive

HONORÉ Daumier was best known in his lifetime as a social satirist. His cartoons, published in left-wing magazines, made his name. However, he was determined to succeed as an artist outside the limitations of satirical drawing.

Daumier's works were lauded only after his death. With the new-found interest in Expressionism at the end of the nineteenth century, and with the advent of Impressionism, Daumier's style found appreciative critics, who cited his works as having been an inspiration to both artistic movements.

Toward the end of his life Daumier's sight deteriorated, and he became poverty-stricken. His slide into destitution was curbed only by the intervention of Corot (1796–1875), who generously provided Daumier with a home.

In an age when Realism required minute attention to detail and "finish," it is easy to see why *The Laundress,* and other work in a similar style by Daumier, with its blurred outlines and indistinct facial features, was not well received in his lifetime. His subject matter, showing an everyday scene from the life of a lower-class woman, is reminiscent of works by Edgar Degas (1834–1917), such as *Women Ironing* (1884).

Realist

JEAN-BAPTISTE-CAMILLE COROT (1796–1875)

THE WOMAN OF THE PEARL

Louvre, Paris. Celimage.sa/Lessing Archive

FRENCH-BORN Corot spent much of his life in Paris, although, like most artists of his era, he made visits to Italy between 1825 and 1835 to study the Old Masters. Unusually, Corot did not choose painting as a career until he reached his mid-20s. This was a decision influenced by fellow Frenchman Achille Etna Michallon (1796–1822), who guided Corot's early career and was himself a renowned landscape artist.

Corot is best known for his landscapes, which were in great demand from the wealthy patrons who supported him. His early paintings were strongly influenced by the Classical tradition of Arcadian landscapes, but works such as *Ville d'Avray* (c.1870) were inspired by the French countryside, marking a move away from the Italian landscapes of his youth toward a more realistic style.

Corot produced relatively few portrait studies which, although of a consistently high standard, have been a neglected part of his oeuvre. The same applies to his nude figure studies. The dots of pink and yellow flesh tones, used to create light, shadow, and form in the face, also anticipate the Impressionist movement.

ATKINSON GRIMSHAW (1836–1893)

LIVERPOOL QUAY BY MOONLIGHT

Tate Gallery, London. Courtesy of Edimedia

JOHN Atkinson Grimshaw was born in Leeds in 1836. He decided to become a full-time painter and in 1861 he left his job with the Great Northern Railway. However, despite his success and popularity in Leeds, his strict Baptist parents strongly disapproved of his chosen career. On one occasion his mother destroyed all his paints.

Until the early 1870s Grimshaw's paintings were predominantly still lifes, with only a few landscapes of the Leeds area. However, as he developed an interest in painting night scenes, he started to paint landscapes. These included *Liverpool from Wapping* (1875), *Nightfall down the Thames* (1880), and *Prince's Dock, Hull* (1887).

As he focused on depicting city scenes, Grimshaw's works were often marked with a layer of smoke or a descending damp fog as he portrayed the pollution endemic to industrial cities in the late nineteenth century. *Liverpool Quay by Moonlight* (1887) has been painted thus, with a low fog hanging just above the street and buildings. A dim, gray film of color diffuses the lights from the shop windows in the distance. The painting is subtle in terms of its palette and composition, although as a whole the image displays quite a murky and cold scene of the Liverpool quay.

JAMES ABBOT MACNEILL WHISTLER (1834–1903)

PORTRAIT OF THE ARTIST'S MOTHER

Musée d'Orsay, Paris. Celimage.sa/Lessing Archive

IN 1859, after studying in Paris, American-born Whistler moved to London. He became renowned for his personality—charming and hostile by turns—as much as for his art. His work often contained elements from the Japanese art that he brought to prominence in Britain, but he was also influenced by nineteenth-century French and British art. He was also a writer and lecturer, publishing a collection of his essays in *The Gentle Art of Making Enemies* (1890).

Whistler was closely involved in London's artistic and literary circles, associating with Rossetti (1828–82) and Oscar Wilde (1854–1901). In 1878 he sued John Ruskin (1819–1900) for libel after he likened Whistler's work to "a paint pot flung at a canvas." Despite winning the case, Whistler was forced into bankruptcy when costs were awarded against him. He left Britain but eventually returned to settle in London.

Portrait of the Artist's Mother is typical of Whistler's accurate facial portraiture and his use of blocks of color. His subjects were seldom named; instead the works bore titles indicated by the colors worn by the sitter. The alternative title for this picture is *Arrangement in Gray and Black No. 1.*

WINSLOW HOMER (1836–1910)

SUMMER NIGHT

Musée d'Orsay, Paris. Celimage.sa/Lessing Archive

WINSLOW Homer was one of the foremost American Realist artists. He was also an illustrator and journalist. He worked in oils and watercolors and produced etchings. His early paintings are predominantly in oils but, from the early 1880s, he began producing watercolors almost exclusively.

Homer lived for a time in NewYork, but he was always happier by the sea. He traveled to England in 1881, where he spent time painting watercolors of English coastal scenes. In 1881–82, back in America, he bought a house near the Atlantic coast at Prout's Neck, where he lived in isolation. His early paintings had been mainly of rural scenes, but in the mid-1880s he switched to sea pictures, such as *Fog Warning* (1885) and *The Life Line* (1884), both of which portray the sea as an angry, life-threatening force. Homer also had a great talent for producing unsentimental pictures of animals, such as *Fox Hunt* (1893) and *Deer Drinking* (1892).

Summer Night is a haunting yet charming scene of two figures dancing by the seashore. It is nighttime and the sea is iridescent with the sparkling reflection of the moon.

JOHN SINGER SARGENT (1856–1925)

A BOATING PARTY

School of Design, Rhode Island. Celimage.sa/Lessing Archive

SARGENT was an American citizen, although he was born in Italy. He spent much of his youth traveling, before settling in London in 1884. His influences were diverse, ranging from the works of Velázquez (1599–1660) and Frans Hals (c.1582–1666) to his Impressionist contemporaries. His awareness of the most up-to-date movements in French art is unsurprising, since his artistic education was in France, under Carolus-Duran (1838–1917).

In London, Sargent earned fame as a portraitist, receiving more commissions than he could possibly accept. Those he undertook, such as *Eva and Betty Wertheimer* (1901) and *The Misses Vickers* (1886), reveal his genius for recreating facial idiosyncracies, as well as his understanding of the human form. In the later years of his life, however, he was able to return to his first love—landscape painting—when he took extended vacations from London to paint the British countryside. During the First World War he was appointed as the official War Artist. The horrors of war are evoked in his disturbing work, *Gassed* (1918).

A Boating Party captures a relaxed scene of boating in New England at the end of the nineteenth century. It is resonant of the French Impressionist style of Renoir or Monet.

Realist

IGNACE HENRI JEAN FANTIN-LATOUR
(1836–1904)

ROSES IN A BOWL

Musée d'Orsay, Paris. Celimage.sa/Lessing Archive

FANTIN-LATOUR was born in Grenoble, France, of an Italian father and Russian mother. His father, also an artist, tutored the young Fantin-Latour for the first years of his life. At the age of 14, he was enrolled in art school and later became a pupil of Courbet (1819–77). Elements of Courbet's technique, along with that of Corot (1796–1875), Delacroix (1798–1863), Titian (c.1487–1576), and Veronese (c.1528–88), can be found in Fantin-Latour's work, although his subject matter differed from theirs. He is best known for his flower studies, although he painted occasional portrait groups as well as historical scenes and landscapes.

Fantin-Latour traveled a little in Europe, but always returned to France. He was prominent in the intellectual and artistic society of late nineteenth-century France—being on good terms with Whistler (1834–1903), Manet (1832–83), and all the Impressionist artists—yet he retained his individual style, exhibiting mainly detailed still lifes and never taking up the lucrative profession of society portraitist.

Roses in a Bowl demonstrates Fantin-Latour's meticulous technique: the gently frilled petals, each formed by a single stroke of paint, are almost photographic in their realism.

THOMAS COWPERTHWAIT EAKINS
(1844–1916)

PORTRAIT OF CLARA J. MATHER

Musée d'Orsay, Paris. Celimage.sa/Scala Archives

EAKINS was born in the US and studied at the Pennsylvania Academy. In the mid-1860s he traveled to Europe, where he was deeply influenced by the art he encountered, in particular that of Velázquez (1599–1660). In 1870, Eakins returned home and became a director of the Pennsylvania Academy, a post from which he later resigned after a scandal caused by his insistence that female students should draw the male figure from nude models.

Eakins was based in Philadelphia for most of his life. From 1866 to 1870 he lived in Europe, studying in Paris. His portraiture was observant and compassionate, for which he acknowledged a debt to Velázquez. Eakins's passion for realism led him to study anatomy and make full use of Edward Muybridge's photographic innovations. His wife, Susan Hannah Macdowell Eakins (1851–1938), whom he married in 1884, was also an artist and photographer. The *Portrait of Clara J. Mather* is a delicate and sensitive masterpiece in whch the artist relies upon simple light and expression to convey purity and beauty.

Today Eakins is regarded as one of the greatest American painters.

Realist

ÉDOUARD MANET (1832–83)

LUNCHEON ON THE GRASS

Musée d'Orsay, Paris. Celimage.sa/Lessing Archive

MANET was born in Paris to wealthy parents and his artistic talents were apparent early in his life. In 1850, after a short stint in the French navy, he joined the studio of Thomas Couture (1815–79), a Neoclassical painter who steered his students away from obsessive attention to detail.

Manet's work was remarkable for its modernity, both in terms of technique and subject matter—qualities that attracted the admiration of a younger group of painters who came to be known as the Impressionists. Despite challenging the views of the art establishment, Manet craved official acceptance for his work. Consequently, he never exhibited with the Impressionists, although his work influenced their development. Manet spent much time with members of the Impressionist group in the cafés of Paris, and during the 1870s he painted in an Impressionist style. Much of his subject matter was also in keeping with the spirit of his contemporary Edgar Degas (1834–1917).

Luncheon on the Grass marked a turning point in French painting. Based on a work by the Italian Old Master Giorgione (c.1477–1510), it caused a scandal in the art world because of the way it challenged Classical motifs.

In 1883, Manet's achievements were recognized by the state when he was awarded the Légion d'honneur.

EUGÈNE BOUDIN (1824–98)

THE BEACH AT TROUVILLE

Musée d'Orsay, Paris. Celimage.sa/Lessing Archive

BOUDIN was apprenticed to a printer in Le Havre and painted in his spare time. However, after visiting northern France and Flanders in 1848 and exhibiting two of his pictures, he enrolled at the École des Beaux-Arts in Paris, where he studied from 1851 to 1853. He exhibited at the Salon of 1859, where his work was admired by Symbolist poet Charles Baudelaire (1821–67).

Boudin was a follower of French landscape and figure painter Jean-Baptiste-Camille Corot (1796–1875), and spent most of his career painting along the coast of northern France. He was one of the first artists to advocate painting in the open air (rather than sketching outside and producing a finished composition in the studio), an idea he introduced to Claude Monet (1840–1926) in 1858. Boudin's work was an extremely important influence on the early career of Monet.

From 1870, Boudin's brushwork became broader. In his later years, he began to use brighter, richer colors. From 1862 he was a regular visitor to Trouville, where he painted this composition of the French upper classes at leisure by the sea. *The Beach at Trouville* has many features that are typical of Boudin's work, including the use of small figures, the lack of a central subject, the play of light on the water, and the broad, atmospheric sky.

Impressionist

BERTHE MORISOT (1841–95)

IN A PARK

Musée du Petit Palais, Paris. Celimage.sa/Lessing Archive

MORISOT, the daughter of a top civil servant and great-great-niece of the Rococo artist Jean-Honoré Fragonard (1732–1806), grew up in a cultured environment. Between 1860 and 1862 she was a pupil of French landscape painter Jean-Baptiste-Camille Corot (1796–1875), who advised her to paint out of doors. She came into contact with the Impressionists through Édouard Manet (1832–83), whom she befriended in 1869. She married Manet's brother and persuaded Manet to experiment with painting outside, to abandon his predominant use of black, and to adopt a lighter, Impressionist palette.

Morisot exhibited at all but one of the Impressionist exhibitions. She excelled at portraits and domestic scenes, which she imbued with a spontaneity and light, airy quality. She always worked in the Impressionist style and had a rare understanding of tonal harmony. She was also highly skilled in the use of watercolors.

Women artists in the nineteenth century were limited in the subject matter they were allowed to paint. That is why the female Impressionists often painted women and children. Morisot was no exception to this, and we see her artistic ability in her painting *In a Park*, where, with quick, vigorous flecks of color she demonstrates her highly distinctive style.

FRÉDÉRIC BAZILLE (1841–70)

THE ARTIST'S STUDIO

Musée d'Orsay, Paris. Celimage.sa/Lessing Archive

BAZILLE came from a middle-class family in the Languedoc region of southern France. In 1859 he began medical studies in Montpellier. Continuing his studies in Paris in 1862, he also took up painting at the studio of Charles Gleyre (1808–74), studying alongside Claude Monet, Pierre-Auguste Renoir (1884–1919), and Alfred Sisley (1839–99). The group often traveled to locations outside Paris to paint in the open air.

In 1864, Bazille gave up medicine and took up painting full time. He shared studios with both Monet and Renoir and first exhibited at the Salon of 1866. His varied work is characterized by its bright colors and limpid atmosphere. Tragically, he died in the Franco-Prussian War (1870–71) before Impressionism had been fully developed. His influences included Édouard Manet (1832–83) and Gustave Courbet (1819–77); some of his subject matter, such as the nude study in *After the Bath* (1870), although clearly influenced by the Old Masters, suggests his willingness to take a more modern approach.

Painted the year he died, *The Artist's Studio* shows Bazille experimenting with an unusual group composition, in which he was heavily influenced by the Japanese prints becoming available in Paris at about this time.

ALFRED SISLEY (1839–99)

THE FOOTBRIDGE AT ARGENTEUIL

Musée d'Orsay, Paris. Celimage.sa/Lessing Archive

ALFRED Sisley was English but was born in Paris, to wealthy parents. He had planned to be a businessman but in 1857 began to draw. In 1862 he met Monet, Bazille, and Renoir at Charles Gleyre's studio in Paris. With them, he painted in the open air in the woods near Barbizon.

An enthusiastic follower of Monet, Sisley was a committed landscape artist. Of all the Impressionists, he experimented the least with his style and technique, painting in the same manner throughout his career, although there is a more brittle quality to his later work. Sisley's main focus was to paint the landscape around him, usually seen from a distance and disappearing to a vanishing point on the horizon.

Sisley died of cancer in 1899, and his finances were in such a poor state that his fellow artists made a collection for his children. At a posthumous auction of his works, however, the prices—so low in his lifetime—rose dramatically.

The informal brushwork in this painting varies in style and technique, according to Sisley's belief that a painting should exhibit a variety of treatment, corresponding to the needs of the subject matter and the effect being sought. This is one reason why Impressionist paintings create such a feeling of vitality.

EDGAR DEGAS (1834–1917)

REPETITION D'UN BALLET SUR LA SCÈNE

Metropolitan Museum of Art, MOMA, New York. Celimage.sa/Lessing Archive

EDGAR Degas came from a wealthy family and trained initially as a historical painter. However, his interest in modern motifs became apparent in the early 1860s, when he began to paint racecourses. He was also a gifted portrait painter, showing a rare insight into the character of his sitters. From early on, Degas's work is almost abstract in its concern for design and pattern and its use of unusual viewpoints. In 1869, he exhibited at the official Paris Salon for the last time, exhibiting independently thereafter.

Degas was instrumental in organizing the first independent Impressionist exhibition in 1874 and was involved in all but one of their subsequent exhibitions. Many of his contemporary motifs proved offensive to the public. At the Impressionist exhibition of 1886 his pastels of women at their toilette (perfectly acceptable in a Classical setting) caused uproar. This painting is an example of Degas's pictures of dancers. He used them to express pattern and movement, often repeating poses drawn from memory or traced from earlier sketches. He often combined several media—this oil painting shows traces of watercolor and pastel. His work was influenced by Japanese prints and the new medium of photography.

From the 1890s, as his eyesight began to deteriorate, Degas painted loose images in pastel, and produced models in wax.

GUSTAVE CAILLEBOTTE (1848–94)

PONT DE L'EUROPE

Petit Palais, Geneva. Celimage.sa/Lessing Archive

A NAVAL engineer and amateur painter, Caillebotte studied as a portraitist and historical painter. He met Edgar Degas (1834–1917) and Pierre-Auguste Renoir (1841–1919) in 1874. He came from a wealthy family and throughout his career supported the other Impressionists, in particular by helping to finance exhibitions and buying many of the canvases himself. Caillebotte's early work bears affinities with that of Édouard Manet (1832–83) and Degas, both Realist painters of city life. Like Manet, Caillebotte's figures are part of his modern setting and not simply vehicles for the effects of light and color, as with other Impressionist painters.

His works are notable for their interesting compositions, often viewed from unusual angles and with part of the image "cut off," as if in a photograph. Until the 1880s, Caillebotte took his images from the world around him— street scenes, family portraits, working-class life, and scenes on the River Yerres where he took vacations. His work became more Impressionist in style and in 1882 he retired from public life, painting only landscapes and still lifes.

This painting is interesting for its composition, with movement in and out of the painting. The dog walks away from the viewer while the couple appear to be walking out of the picture.

PIERRE-AUGUSTE RENOIR (1841–1919)

BAL DU MOULIN DE LA GALETTE, MONTMARTRE

Musée d'Orsay, Paris. Celimage.sa/Lessing Archive

RENOIR, who began his career a porcelain painter, was a founder member of Impressionism, with Monet, in 1860. Bazille and Alfred Sisley soon joined the group and from 1863 they began to work out of doors near Barbizon, where Renoir also befriended Camille Pissarro (1830–1903) and Paul Cézanne (1839–1906).

He exhibited at the first three Impressionist exhibitions and at the seventh. Otherwise, he showed his work at private one-man exhibitions and at the Paris Salon. Until the 1890s, Renoir was generally more interested in painting people than landscapes. Unlike some of the other Impressionists, he favored society portraits and pictures of the middle classes at play. He painted with soft, caressing, almost sensual brushstrokes—there is no trace of the darker undertones found in the work of Édouard Manet (1832–83) and Edgar Degas (1834–1917).

Renoir became dissatisfied with his style and in 1881 traveled to North Africa and Italy. For a few years he practiced a harder, more "Classical" style, in which forms were far more clearly delineated and the brushwork less free.

From about 1890 he returned to his softer style, and painted mainly nudes and landscapes. In 1900 he was awarded the Légion d'honneur and his work was increasingly shown abroad.

Impressionist

MARY CASSATT (1844–1926)

YOUNG WOMAN SEWING IN THE GARDEN

Musée d'Orsay, Paris. Celimage.sa/Lessing Archive

MARY Cassatt, a wealthy American artist, studied at the Pennsylvania Academy of Arts between 1861 and 1865. She came to Paris in 1866. She first exhibited at the official Salon in 1868. She toured Italy during the Franco-Prussian War (1870–71). She exhibited at the Paris Salon in 1872 and traveled in Europe during 1873, when she encountered the work of Velázquez (1599–1660), Rembrandt (1606–69), and Rubens (1577–1640)— superb colorists whom she greatly admired.

Cassatt was introduced to Edgar Degas (1834–1917) in 1877; both he and Renoir (1841–1919) were important influences on her work. She took part in several of the independent Impressionist exhibitions in Paris and introduced the Impressionists to several wealthy American collectors.

She painted in oils and from 1890 also produced high-quality prints, making effective use of her understanding of line and drawing. She is particularly known for her insightful pictures of women, often with their children. This painting is fairly typical in its content and style, but note how Cassatt implies height in such a way that the background seems like a flat-patterned backdrop—undoubtedly a skill learned from Degas.

CAMILLE PISSARRO (1830–1903)

WOMAN HANGING UP THE WASHING

Musée d'Orsay, Paris. Celimage.sa/Lessing Archive

PISSARRO was born in the West Indies, although he had Danish nationality. The oldest of the Impressionists, he went to Paris in 1885, where he painted in the manner of the landscapist Gustave Courbet (1819–77). He was a founder member of the Impressionist group, and the only one to exhibit at all eight independent exhibitions. From 1888, he suffered eye problems and stopped working in the open air. Instead, he concentrated on views of city life, usually painted looking down from hotel windows. In 1889, with the other Impressionists, he exhibited at the Paris World Fair. During the 1890s his work became increasingly well known.

Between the mid-1880s and 1890, under the influence of Georges Seurat (1859–91), Pissarro painted in the "scientific" divisionist or pointillist style. From the 1880s, he began to concentrate on figures as the subjects of his work. *Woman Hanging up the Washing* shows Pissarro's new style and the dabs of color used in pointillism. However, although achieving a monumentality of sorts, he does not adhere to the pointillist system and his work retains the freshness and spontaneity so typical of Impressionism.

ARMAND GUILLAUMIN (1841–1927)

SOLEIL COUCHANT À IVRY

Musée d'Orsay, Paris. Celimage.sa/Lessing Archive

ARMAND Guillaumin was working in his uncle's shop when he began to attend evening drawing classes at the age of 15. In 1861 he began to make use of the facilities at the Académie Suisse where, for a small fee, artists could paint nude models provided by the atelier. It was here that he met Pissarro and Cézanne.

Although he has never been regarded as a major Impressionist painter, Guillaumin was involved from the beginning when, like many of the group, he was rejected at the Salon of 1863 and exhibited at the Salon des Refusés.

Under the influence of Pissarro, Guillaumin, like Cézanne at this time, took up the Impressionist way of painting and often painted out-of-doors—often at Pontoise, where Pissarro lived. The three still remained friends and Cézanne once even copied a painting of Guillaumin's which showed workers shoveling sand.

Guillaumin is known for landscapes around Paris and along the Seine. This is a view of Ivry, an industrial suburb of Paris, in which he combines the glorious blue heights of the sky and the sun's golden rays with the factory chimneys' billowing smoke.

JOAQUIN SOROLLA (1863–1923)

A WALK ON THE BEACH

Museo Sorolla, Madrid. Celimage.sa/Lessing Archive

JOAQUIN Sorolla was the leading Spanish Impressionist painter and has become an increasingly popular figure within the pantheon of Impressionism. He began to paint as a boy, receiving tutoring from the age of fifteen. His extensive training included art school in Madrid and four years of tuition in Rome. Sorolla's extraordinary mastery of the depiction of light and the effects of light characterizes his works. He manages to capture both the context and the character of his subjects.

His greatest works compare in style with Singer Sargent and Winslow Homer. Like them, Sorolla favored elegant figurative portraits more often in full length, with flowing dresses displaying a slight breeze rustling through the fabric. Another favorite subject for Sorolla was the beaches of his beloved Valencia, where he depicted relaxed and playful scenes of children, set against gently crashing waves. Sorolla deployed shadow and tint of color, with a freedom that was to mark the end of Realism in Spanish painting. His informality was disarming, and he would often gather family members to be the subjects of his works.

CLAUDE MONET (1840–1926)

BLUE WATER LILIES

Musée d'Orsay, Paris. Celimage.sa/Lessing Archive

CLAUDE Monet was born in Le Havre. In 1859 he moved to Paris, where he met Bazille, Pissarro, Sisley, and Renoir. They soon began painting together outdoors. Unlike Manet and Degas, Monet was not concerned with painting the realities of life. His interest lay in nature and the fleeting, natural effects of light. His few paintings of interiors and of city life were vehicles for the study of light in a different environment.

Success was long in coming and for many years his family suffered hardship. His first wife, Camille, died of cancer in 1879 and thereafter he lived with Alice Hoschedé, the wife of a bankrupt former patron.

Monet is best known for his series paintings, in which he explored particular subjects in differing light conditions at various times of day, most famously his haystacks, poplar trees, and Rouen Cathedral. His water lilies, produced almost exclusively from 1899 when he moved to Giverny, outside Paris, are a natural progression of this. As his eyesight deteriorated, his work became increasingly abstract, as here, with almost everything except the lilies and the reflective surface of the water eliminated.

PIERRE PUVIS DE CHAVANNES (1824–98)

POOR FISHERMAN

Celimage.sa/Lessing Archive

FRENCH-BORN Puvis de Chavannes studied in Italy with Delacroix. As a result, his monumentally scaled work had more in common with Italian Renaissance frescoes than with contemporary French Impressionist painting. His huge, mural-like canvases were admired by Symbolist poets Charles Baudelaire and Stéphane Mallarmé (1842–98), and his boldly flat, decorative style was adopted by Gauguin and painters of the Nabi school.

The Symbolists used painting to express social comment, often combined with religious overtones, which endowed art with a sense of inner necessity, or objective meaning—a concept that led to the development of Abstract art. In *Poor Fisherman*, the simple linear effect and pale, almost monotone, palette anticipate Pablo Picasso's (1881–1973) "blue" period, which was undoubtedly influenced by Puvis de Chavannes's work. When the picture was first exhibited it was attacked for its unnatural, anaemic colors. The weak light falls down the center of the painting, while the rest of the scene is plunged into gloom, with the exception of the light-flooded figure of the baby. Puvis de Chavannes quickly won the admiration of Impressionists and Aesthetes, who admired his apparent disregard for the prevailing artistic trend toward Realism and his development of Symbolist notions of dreams and visions.

GUSTAVE MOREAU (1826–98)

GALATEA

Musée d'Orsay, Paris. Celimage.sa/Lessing Archive

A CLASSICALLY trained academic artist, Moreau was a major force in the creation of the Symbolist movement. His intense, magical paintings were often inspired by visions. As a teacher at the École des Beaux-Arts in Paris, his views on color had a profound impact on his pupil Henri Matisse (1869–1954), as well as on the Fauves and Surrealists.

The Symbolist movement was allied to Aestheticism, which developed early Romantic ideals combined with a taste for the morbid, represented in Britain by Aubrey Beardsley (1872–1898) and Oscar Wilde (1845–1900). Moreau was criticized for his pseudo-Romantic tricks, exemplified by his interest in the femme fatale.

In *Galatea*, Moreau explores the symbolic potential of a favorite mythological siren. According to legend, the nymph Galatea fell in love with a humble shepherd, Acis, but was pursued by a Cyclops who had fallen in love with her. In order to escape, she turned Acis into a river and dived into the water. In this brooding piece, the "dream state" is not a representation of the subconscious, as in twentieth-century Surrealism; rather, it is triggered by sensual experience and represents an escape from the mundane.

ODILON REDON (1840–1916)

ANEMONES AND LILACS IN A BLUE VASE

Musée du Petit Palais, Paris. Celimage.sa/Lessing Archive

FRENCH artist and writer Odilon Redon began his artistic life as a Realist landscape painter, influenced by Courbet and Corot. By the 1880s and 1890s he was hailed as the quintessential Symbolist artist. He knew the Symbolist poets Baudelaire and Mallarmé, and, in common with the movement's other artists, his work reflected Symbolist literature. The Symbolists' 1886 manifesto repudiated the Impressionists' visual emphasis on nature—preferring contemplation of the realities of the imagination by the use of symbolism, patterns, and images. The spiritual dimension of their work often had political meaning, and sometimes verged on anarchism.

Redon was fascinated with expressions of mysticism and influenced the Nabis painters with the flat-patterned charcoal drawings and lithography of his later years. The Nabis school had an effect on the Abstract movement through Surrealist painters such as Francis Picabia (1878–1953).

Redon was an outstanding exponent of vibrant still lifes. His delicate and bright flowers have a warm and refreshing quality.

GUSTAV KLIMT (1862–1918)

THE KISS

Osterreichische Gallery, Vienna. Celimage.sa/Lessing Archive

KLIMT was the founding father and a leading member of the Vienna Secession movement, a group of artists who consciously rejected the academic style of the late nineteenth century. He was celebrated for rich, complex, gold-dazzling friezes and portraits of powerful, chic women from Vienna's turn-of-the-century society. Klimt's artistic vocabulary drew on a wealth of Symbolist imagery, incorporating esoteric design and eroticism. Because of this, his work did not always find favor within the Viennese art world.

Instead, Klimt found extensive patronage abroad, completing the famous Belgian Stoclet Frieze in 1911. This Art Nouveau masterpiece, made for the Wiener Werkstätte arts and crafts guild movement, was influenced by William Morris and Charles Rennie Mackintosh (1868–1928). His early work included impressionistic landscape studies, painted during vacations in the Austrian Alps.

Klimt's exquisite language reached its artistic culmination in his seminal work *The Kiss*, a celebration of his deeply-held belief in the transforming power of idealized love. The painting was produced after Klimt's visit to the Byzantine mosaics in Ravenna, Italy, and was one of his few "Golden Period" pieces to survive the ravages of a Nazi fire at the end of the Second World War. His later work was a powerful influence on the German Expressionism of Egon Schiele (1890–1918) and Oskar Kokoschka (1886–1980).

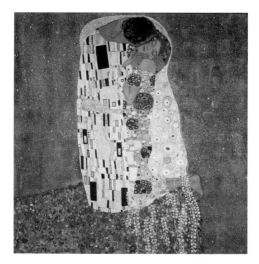

DUNCAN GRANT (1885-1978)

JAMES STRACHEY

Tate Gallery, London. Courtesy of Edimedia

DUNCAN Grant was the son of a Scottish army officer. He moved to India with his parents and lived there until the age of nine. He studied with Jacques-Emile Blanche in Paris in 1906, and then at the Slade School of Art, London. He befriended and worked alongside artists such as Roger Fry and Vanessa Bell. Through their mutual commitment to the decorative arts and painting, they became codirectors of the Omega Workshops in 1913.

In the 1920s and 1930s Grant was arguably the most famous British artist in the world. His work incorporated a range of media and methods. He designed fabrics, china, interiors, murals, and costumes.

His lovers included Adrian Stephen, John Maynard Keynes, and David Garnett, although his cousin, Lytton Strachey, also courted him. Though he was homosexual throughout his life, he fathered the child of Vanessa Bell, Angelica, and lived with the Bell family at Charleston Farm in East Sussex for many years.

Duncan Grant was a member of the Camden Town Group, who were inspired by Walter Sickert's dark and impressionistic paintings, and his engravings of this working-class section of London. This portrait of James Strachey (brother to Lytton), with its dark palette of red and black, clearly demonstrates the influence of Sickert.

AMEDEO MODIGLIANI (1884–1920)

RECLINING FEMALE NUDE

Museum of Modern Art, New York. Celimage.sa/Lessing Archive

AN Italian painter, sculptor, and draftsman, Modigliani worked mainly in Paris. He studied the Italian Renaissance and is often seen as heir to Botticelli because of the linear grace of his long, slender figures.

From 1906 he became a familiar figure around the nightspots of Montmartre. He was influenced by African sculpture and Cubism, and by the work of Paul Cézanne (1839–1906) and Pablo Picasso (1881–1973). In 1909 he met the sculptor Constantin Brancusi (1876–1957) and for the next five years spent the majority of his time carving. But with the start of the First World War in 1914, materials were hard to come by so he resumed painting. His subject matter was almost exclusively portraits of his friends and erotic female nudes. His models were often poor, and he depicted them with tenderness. He used broad blocks of color, but color was never the guiding spirit of his art, which was dependent on the purity and expressive quality of his draftsmanship.

Modigliani lived a penurious life, despite his great talent, and died from tuberculosis in 1920—a disease not helped by his dissolute lifestyle. "I am going to drink myself dead," he said, and promptly did. His mistress Jeanne Hébuterne, who was pregnant with his second child, committed suicide on the day of his funeral.

GEORGES SEURAT (1859–91)

BATHING AT ASNIÈRES

The National Gallery, London. Celimage.sa/Lessing Archive

SEURAT came from a wealthy background and was a highly intelligent, methodical man. He started to paint in about 1881 and exhibited at the last Impressionist exhibition in 1886.

Like many young painters at the time, Seurat learned from Impressionism and then moved on. He was fascinated by the science of light and color theory, and sought to create a rational, formal art through the application of rules, using color and line in a prescribed form to create color and light effects. The style he developed used the primary colors of the spectrum, placed in tiny dots onto a flat, colored background so that the colors became mixed in the eye of the viewer. Hence, yellow and blue placed close together on the canvas would appear as green when viewed from a distance. This technique was known as pointillism, or divisionism, and was also practiced by Paul Signac (1863–1935) and Camille Pissarro (1830–1903).

Bathing at Asnières is an early work and Seurat's first large-scale composition. It shares its subject matter and palette with the Impressionists but its static, monumental quality is reminiscent of the early Renaissance artist Piero della Francesca (c.1416–92).

Seurat died suddenly at the age of 31, probably from meningitis; by this time he was the acknowledged leader of the avant-garde.

VINCENT VAN GOGH (1853–90)

SUNFLOWERS

The National Gallery, London. Celimage.sa/Lessing Archive

VAN GOGH discovered his artistic vocation in 1880, having worked previously as an art dealer and a lay preacher. Vincent lived and painted in the Netherlands until 1885, producing dark images of peasants that emphasized the hardship of their lives. In 1886, he moved to Paris and his palette became brighter and more intense.

In 1888 van Gogh settled in Arles in the south of France, but the years 1888–90 were tumultuous for him. He quarrelled with Paul Gauguin (1848–1903), with whom he had hoped to set up an artists' cooperative, and cut off his own ear. Subsequently he spent time in an asylum at Saint-Rémy before moving to Auvers in 1880 to be near his brother, Theo, who supported him financially all his life. However, on July 29 1890 he committed suicide. He left over 800 paintings and drawings; his work had an enormous influence on Expressionism, Fauvism, and Abstract Art.

Van Gogh was a psychologically tortured individual and this is reflected in the intensity of his work. He became obsessed with the power of color as a symbol and evolved his own style of great swirling brushstrokes. This version of *Sunflowers* (one of many) was painted during van Gogh's stay in Arles before his decline into insanity. The entire canvas is based on broad, thickly painted areas of yellows and browns.

HENRI DE TOULOUSE-LAUTREC (1864–1901)

LA REVUE BLANCHE

Musée Toulouse-Lautrec, Albi. Celimage.sa/Lessing Archive

TOULOUSE-LAUTREC came from an aristocratic family. In his teens he broke both his legs and they ceased to grow while his torso continued to mature. He began to paint in the studio of Léon Bonnat (1833–1922) in 1882 and had his own studio in Montmartre at the age of 21.

His early influence was the Impressionists—particularly Degas, who shared his interest in theater performers and his fascination with prints by Japanese artists Hokusai (1760–1849) and Hiroshige (1797–1858). Likewise, Lautrec also painted brothels, living in one in 1894, and racecourses.

Van Gogh, whom he met in 1886, was another influence, notably for his use of cross-hatching. Gauguin's use of broad, flat color and graphic outlines also influenced the posters and lithographs that Lautrec began to produce from the 1890s, and which brought him instant recognition. *La Revue Blanche* is one of these posters, designed to promote the artificial nightlife of Paris.

Lautrec became an alcoholic and died young, either from the effects of alcoholism or the syphilis he contracted in his 20s.

PAUL GAUGUIN (1848–1903)

WOMAN WITH A FLOWER

Carlsberg Glyptotek, Copenhagen. Celimage.sa/Lessing Archive

PAUL Gauguin, the son of a French father and Creole mother, began painting in the early 1870s while working as a stockbroker. In 1883 he became a full-time artist. He exhibited in the last four Impressionist exhibitions, but his painting did not bring financial success. In 1886 he left his family and moved to Pont Aven in Brittany, where he produced *The Vision after the Sermon* (1888), in which he abandoned the Impressionist style, using flat areas of color as a means of expression.

Gauguin moved to Tahiti in 1891, where he believed he became one with nature, a feeling reflected in his later work, which is influenced by the art of primitive peoples. He lived in the South Pacific until his death, returning to France only occasionally.

Woman with a Flower is one of Gauguin's first Tahitian paintings. His model is modestly dressed, revealing the European influence on the local people. In contrast, Gauguin's later paintings, depicting the apparent simplicity of life in the South Seas, were highly romanticized. During the last decade of his life he painted richly colored and stylized pastoral scenes, nudes, and some still lifes, often with symbolic or allegorical overtones.

PAUL SIGNAC (1836–1935)

THE CHÂTEAU DES PAPES, AVIGNON

Musée d'Orsay, Paris. Celimage.sa/Lessing Archive

SIGNAC began his career as an Impressionist but met Seurat in 1884, when they both exhibited at the first exhibition of the Société des Artistes Indépendants. He contributed to all nine exhibitions and became president of the society in 1908.

Signac became a friend of Seurat and a follower of his pointillist technique. Signac took on his mantle after Seurat died suddenly in 1891, and became the r ecognized leader of the Neoimpressionists—a term coined by the critic Félix Fénéon to signify the group of artists who had been influenced by the Impressionists but who had then moved on to different styles. Signac's palette became increasingly bright and his style less technical. From the 1890s, his style was more decorative and artificial than scientific. In 1899 he published *From Delacroix to Neoimpressionism*, which was considered the definitive work on the subject of Pointillism, although it was more a defence of the style than an accurate history.

After 1900 he abandoned Pointillism and began to use small, square dabs of color. This technique was used to paint *The Château des Papes, Avignon*, which looks as though it is created from pieces of mosaic. Signac executed his paintings in the studio, working from watercolor studies done on site.

PAUL CÉZANNE (1839–1906)

MONT SAINTE-VICTOIRE

Private Collection. Celimage.sa/Lessing Archive

CÉZANNE grew up in Aix-en-Provence and trained as a lawyer. In 1861 he began to study painting at the Académie Suisse in Paris. Between 1862 and 1865, he met and became good friends with several Impressionist painters.

Until about 1870 his work varied in style and motif. In some works he used thick impasto and a palette knife, while for others he used more traditional brushwork; his palette was always dark. Despite these differences in style and content, his work reveals an early interest in the relationships between different planes and the balance between form and color. During this period he painted still lifes, portraits, and semi-historical and erotic subjects, all infused with an internal violence.

Under the influence of his mentor Pissarro, Cézanne painted in the Impressionist style between 1870–79. From 1880, however, he developed a new style. He applied paint in repeated parallel brushstrokes to produce a subtle, almost woven, effect. He painted many empty landscapes, including a series of paintings showing Mont Sainte-Victoire, near his home in Aix. He also painted portraits and still lifes, in which he experimented with perspective. Although he never lost sight of his subject matter, Cézanne's work looked forward to the abstraction of the twentieth century and had a huge influence on future generations of artists.

AUGUSTE RODIN (1840–1917)

SAINT JOHN BAPTIST

Musée d'Orsay, Paris. Celimage.sa/Lessing Archive

AUGUSTE Rodin was the most celebrated French sculptor of the nineteenth century. His works were extraordinary for their realism and expressiveness. His sensitive modeling and ability to render movement through the play of light on a sculpted surface were unsurpassed.

Rodin became assistant sculptor at the Sèvres Porcelain Factory in 1864. In 1875, he studied Michelangelo's work in Italy and began to apply elements of his technique— in particular, leaving some areas smooth and others unworked—to his own work. This was the turning point of his career. *The Age of Bronze* (1876) caused controversy at the Salon of 1877 because the figure was deemed so lifelike that he was accused of having taken a cast from a live model. Rodin also introduced the concept of producing a fragment of the body, such as a head, as a finished piece. His sculptures were the cause of dissent and several commissions were rejected.

Saint John Baptist is an unflattering, roughly modeled figure that critics derided as improper and shocking. Yet the image of physical strength is appropriate for the saint, an ascetic who lived and preached in the desert.

WILLIAM COLDSTREAM (1908-87)

MRS INEZ SPENDER

Tate Gallery, London. Courtesy of Edimedia

WILLIAM Coldstream was one of the most influential men in British art during the twentieth century, recognized for both his paintings and his teachings.

Mrs Spender is quite obviously the focus of the artist in this painting, and quite unusually he has captured her entire frame, not just her head and shoulders. The subject is outstretched on her chair. Yet her pose is not especially relaxed, as suggested through her expression and her hands, which are wrapped closely around her waist.

In his portrait of Inez Spender, Coldstream adopts a demure and soft palette. The sitter's face has been described with an almost photographic realism, whereas the sofa she rests on, and the wall behind her, are loosely outlined in their forms. Coldstream subtly combines the effects of Impressionism and Realism in this canvas.

The warm brown haze that distills the entire image gives the painting an authentic appearance. It looks as though it could be an old photograph, which has been subjected to the effects of natural light and time.

ÉDOUARD VUILLARD (1868–1940)

TWO GIRLS WALKING

FRENCH painter Vuillard studied at the Parisian Académie Julian, where he met Pierre Bonnard (1867–1947) and other Nabis group members. He shared a studio with Bonnard; both were affected by Gauguin's Pont-Aven group, with its concentration on flat blocks of color rather than the traditional three-dimensional approach. Fellow Nabi painter Maurice Denis's (1870–1943) belief that a picture, "before being a horse, nude, or subject is essentially a flat surface covered with colors in a certain order," was also very influential on Vuillard's work.

Vuillard favored the settings of interior scenes and urban landscapes, which allowed him to reproduce their subtle atmosphere with the use of strong surface patterns. He was influenced by the interest in Japanese prints and, although his work has suffered comparisons with Bonnard's daring lyricism, he created vibrant, poetic, and often extremely sensual paintings.

The intense, vibrant colors of *Two Girls Walking* capture a moment of girlhood togetherness within a decorative patchwork of structural forms. The modest scene and apparent simplicity of style obscures the technical mastery of the piece.

Nabis

PIERRE BONNARD (1867–1947)

THE TERRACE AT VERNON

FRENCH painter Bonnard studied in Paris, where he met Vuillard and other members of the Nabis group (*nabi* is the Hebrew word for "prophet"). The group developed from Paul Gauguin's Brittany-based Pont-Aven school, which concentrated on flat-patterned composition. The Nabis first exhibited at the Café Volpini in 1889, when Bonnard received acclaim for his early graphic work, in particular his screen printing, in which the influences of Art Nouveau and Japanese prints were apparent. He advocated the Nabis doctrine of abandoning three-dimensional representation in favor of areas of flat color, although he never truly adopted the movement's Symbolist objectives, preferring to explore the creative implications of observation rather than imagination.

Matisse's celebrated use of color blocking had a powerful influence on Bonnard, leading him to explore the decorative effects of color and eventually resulting in his fluid depiction of light. *The Terrace at Vernon* shows a richly diverse range of effects. These are achieved by the application of Pointillist and Neoimpressionist brushwork to the background. This painting deploys vibrant and shimmering colors and is balanced by attentive light and shade effects.

Nabis

EDVARD MUNCH (1863–1944)

THE SCREAM

Nasjonalgalleriet, Oslo ©DACS 2003; Edvard Munch/Celimage.sa/Lessing Archive

THE work of Norwegian artist Munch is often regarded as a bridge between the Post-impressionists, such as van Gogh and Gauguin, and the early-twentieth-century German Expressionist movement. Indeed, his work was an important influence on the development of the Expressionist movement. Munch studied art at Oslo in 1880–82, and during visits to Paris and Berlin came into contact with the artistic innovations that helped shape his own theories and style of painting.

Munch's paintings, although ostensibly portraying reality, use distortion and exaggerated color to express an interior world. His work displays the turbulent emotions that would lead to a nervous breakdown in 1908.

Munch adopted the swirling, intensely colored style of van Gogh to give his work psychological force and passion. The eddying brushstrokes create visual echoes all around his figures, and can be seen in *The Madonna* (1894–95). They help to imbue works such as *The Scream* with a feeling of angst, expressing a destructive energy that is barely contained. *The Scream* is part of three groups of work on the themes of love, suffering, and death, which Munch called collectively the *Frieze of Life*.

Expressionist

PAULA MODERSOHN-BECKER (1876–1907)

OLD WOMAN, SITTING, WITH CAT

BORN in Dresden, Modersohn-Becker studied art but, at her family's insistence, also trained as a teacher. While studying in Berlin from 1896 to 1898 she met members of an artistic colony who lived in a farming village, Worswede, near Bremen. Modersohn-Becker met her future husband, Otto, at the colony when she moved there in 1898. She died from an embolism, three weeks after the birth of her daughter.

Modersohn-Becker left Worswede three times to stay in Paris, where she came into contact with the work of Cézanne, Gauguin, and van Gogh, all of whom were highly influential on her work. In Gauguin, she found examples of the primitivism for which she strived. Her use of discrete blocks of color is an acknowledgement of her debt to Cézanne, while her animated brushwork is a reminder of the work of van Gogh.

Using these influences, Modersohn-Becker created a style that combines simply depicted forms with a suggestive use of color, applied in concentrated brush strokes. Her main themes were single figure studies or self-portraits, such as this one, completed the year she died. Self-portraits, as vehicles for exploring ideas of the self, were popular among Expressionists.

Expressionist

EGON SCHIELE (1890–1918)

SELF-PORTRAIT WITH RAISED ARMS, REAR VIEW

Private Collection. Celimage.sa/Lessing Archive

SCHIELE was born in Lower Austria. He began studying at the Vienna Academy of Fine Arts in 1906, where he was introduced to the members of the artistic avant-garde. In 1907 he met Gustave Klimt (1862–1918), whose impact on his work was obvious.

Schiele soon began to develop his own painfully personal style and came to be regarded as one of the leading Expressionist artists (although he did not identify himself as such), because of the deeply emotional content of his work, often expressed by distorted figures. Schiele died at the age of 28 in the influenza pandemic that spread across Europe just as he was beginning to receive recognition for his work.

Schiele was fascinated by Freud's writings on the subconscious, which inspired much of the material for his paintings. His main themes were portraits, self-portraits, and nudes, all giving him scope to analyze inner emotions. There was often an overt eroticism and sexuality in his subjects; several of his paintings are sexually explicit and Schiele served a short jail term for obscenity in 1912.

This work shows Schiele in a typically contorted, angular pose.

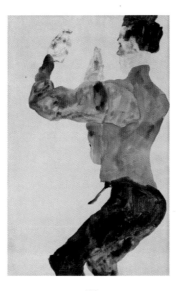

Expressionist

FRANZ MARC (1880–1916)

LITTLE YELLOW HORSES

Staatsgalerie, Stuttgart. Celimage.sa/Lessing Archive

GERMAN artist Franz Marc originally studied theology but turned to art in 1900, studying at Munich University. During his time in Munich, Marc became involved with the German Art Noveau movement, known as Jugendstil. In 1903 and 1907 he visited Paris, where he was particularly affected by the works of van Gogh. In 1911, Marc teamed with Wassily Kandinsky (1866–1944) to found the *Blaue Reiter* (Blue Rider) group, staging exhibitions in 1912 and 1913. Blaue Reiter also published an Almanac containing some of Marc's art theories.

Marc is generally regarded as an exponent of the German Expressionist movement because of his powerful synthesis of color and form, but by the end of his career his work was closer in style to the Abstract movement. His career was cut short in 1914 when he began military service; he was killed at Verdun in 1916.

Marc believed in the spirituality of animals and often used animal subjects as vehicles for his artistic exploration. The combination of the rounded, simplistic forms of the horses and the warmth of the yellows and reds in *Little Yellow Horses* manifests Marc's search for an artistic resolution of form and color, and the depth of his achievement.

ERNST LUDWIG KIRCHNER (1880–1938)

BERLIN STREET SCENE

KIRCHNER was the cofounder of Die Brücke (The Bridge), the first grouping of German Expressionists, based in Dresden, and inspired by Gauguin, van Gogh, Munch, and primitive art. Their art was to be a bridge to the art of the past, aspiring to simplicity in color and form.

Kirchner was the most successful member of the group, becoming possibly the most famous German Expressionist. Largely due to problems caused by his often difficult personality, Die Brücke broke up in 1913. Following a nervous breakdown in 1917, Kirchner moved to Switzerland. Several of his works, along with paintings by van Gogh and Picasso, were exhibited as examples of "Degenerate Art" in a 1937 Nazi exhibition in Munich. Kirchner was deeply upset by this; in 1938 he committed suicide.

By 1911 Die Brücke had moved to Berlin. While there, Kirchner made many paintings of city scenes. In *Berlin Street Scene* the fierce colors produce a shocking contrast. The upward movement of the scene is enhanced by the direction of the deliberately frenzied brushstrokes. The heavily outlined angular forms, typical of Kirchner, suggest constrained yet violent emotion.

Expressionist

MARC CHAGALL (1887–1985)

THE JUGGLER

BORN in Vitebsk, Russia, into a devout Jewish family, Chagall first studied in St Petersburg while working as a sign painter. He moved to Paris in 1910, where he met the Symbolist poet Apollinaire and the Cubists. He was introduced to Robert Delaunay's (1885–1941) Orphists by Delaunay's Russian-born artist wife, Sonia. The Orphists were extending Cubism into a greater color range of circles, segments, and rhythmic patterns, which they called "simultaneity." Chagall returned home on the outbreak of the First World War and joined the pro-French "Knave of Diamonds" group, which rebelled against the Moscow art school's directives. He combined his earlier European influences with a love of his Jewish heritage to develop a very personal, mystical style.

It is hard to categorize Chagall's prolific output, which ranged from Cubist through Expressionist to Surrealist. *The Juggler* probably resulted from Chagall's involvement with the Jewish State Theater during the 1920s. After the 1918 revolution he was made director of Vitebsk Art School, creating an avant-garde center until he was unseated by Malevich. His oeuvre included ballet sets, biblical illustrations, and stained-glass windows.

OSKAR KOKOSCHKA (1886–1980)

THE BRIDE OF THE WIND

KOKOSCHKA was one of the foremost Expressionist painters. He was born in Austria and studied in Vienna from 1905–08, at a time when the city was at the center of cultural innovation, with intellectuals such as Sigmund Freud (1856–1939) and Arnold Schoenberg (1847–1951) working there. In 1910 Kokoschka moved to Berlin to work as a graphic artist on the magazine *Der Sturm* (The Storm), which focused on the art of the German Expressionists. He began to paint what are termed his "psychological portraits": works that seek to illustrate the feelings and emotions of the sitter.

The entire spectrum of emotion is projected from this image, with its chaotic brushstrokes, emotive range of color, and sweeping lines. A similar method and feeling are apparent in Kokoschka's expressive paintings from the First World War. These works became very personal to the artist, full, as they were, of iconographic imagery and symbolism that gave a voice to his concerns. In this work, color becomes as important and prevalent as the subject itself.

Expressionist

ANDRÉ DERAIN (1880–1954)

CHARING CROSS BRIDGE

ONE of the original Fauve group, Derain took up painting against his parents' wishes, first working in his Chatou studio with Maurice de Vlaminck (1876–1958) and then with Fauve leader Henri Matisse (1869–1954) in the south of France. Derain exhibited with the avant-garde group in the famous Salon d'Automne of 1905; the exhibition was brought to Britain by painter-art historian Roger Fry (1866–1934), when the works were labeled for the first time as "Post-impressionist." Derain initially flirted with Neoimpressionism, expressed in the pointillism of Seurat and Pissarro, who applied pure color in small dots in a scientifically based chromatic schema. The technique was subsumed by the Fauves (literally, the "Wild Beasts"), who advanced new conceptual arrangements based on childlike simplicity of form, flat patterns and freedom of line. Under the influence of van Gogh and Gauguin, pure color became all-important.

In *Charing Cross Bridge*, the sensational application of color supersedes any concern for depth of field, as the free-flowing lines add a dynamic distribution of movement. Although fascinated with color, Derain is often seen as the bridge between Matisse and Picasso. He worked alongside Georges Braque (1882–1963) and Picasso studying African and Cézannesque forms, which led to the development of Cubism.

Fauvist

HENRI MATISSE (1869–1954)

THE DANCE II

Hermitage, St . Peterburg ©DACS 2003;Henri Matisse/
Celimage.sa/Lessing Archive

ACKNOWLEDGED as a twentieth-century "great," critics regard Matisse as the revolutionary master of color, while Picasso is the revolutionary master of form. The leader of the Fauves, Matisse stormed onto the art scene in the now celebrated 1905 Salon d'Automne exhibition. He initially studied law, becoming a clerk before he turned to art when his tutor, the Symbolist artist Gustave Moreau, allowed him into the École des Beaux-Arts without taking the entrance examination. Such a late start meant that his skills were more rudimentary than those of his contemporaries, but this gave his work a naive charm that he exploited in his later color experiments. His early works were restrained until he discovered the work of the Pointillists, whose free approach toward color redirected the course of his painting. The celebrated *Luxe, Calme et Volupté* (1904–05) is an experiment in the patterned surfaces that underlined his lifelong search for "balance, purity, and serenity."

During his Post-impressionist phase, Matisse developed structural strength through the study of primitive art. But when Picasso and the Cubists revolutionized the expression of form, Matisse continued to explore how color's decorative effects could dictate form, shape, and light. In this painting, for example, he uses just three colors to create such an incandescent vibrancy that the dancers appear to leap off the canvas.

Fauvist

MAURICE DE VLAMINCK (1876–1958)

RESTAURANT DE LA MACHINE À BOUGIVAL

BORN to Flemish parents, Vlaminck moved to Paris at the age of three. He worked as a writer, busker-violinist, and odd-jobber until, at the age of 23 and with no formal training, he took up painting. Unfettered by the established protocol of formalized Classical art, he relished his freedom of style and sense of energy. He often played on this, only acknowledging van Gogh as an inspiration for his "savage" approach. He shared a studio with André Derain in Chatou on the Seine and became a member of the Fauve group through Derain's connection with Matisse. His wild work, exhibited in the 1905 Salon d'Automne, inspired one critic, who was so angered by the "violent" paintings, to coin the name Les Fauves ("Wild Beasts") to refer to the group.

Vlaminck declared that instinct was the foundation of art. "I try to paint with my heart and loins," he said, proud of calling himself a barbarian. He was the first painter to collect African masks, which added a savage intensity to his style.

A strong Pointillist and Fauvist influence are evident in Vlaminck's *Restaurant de la Machine à Bougival.* The painting is notable for a strong use of color, with heightened tones and a bold presence. The application of red to the canvas provides the image with a dominant feature, and gives it a sense of energy and vibrancy.

RAOUL DUFY (1877–1953)

LES CAVALIERS SOUS BOIS

Centre Pompidou, Musée Nationale d'Art Moderne, Paris.
© DACS 2003; Raoul Dufy/Celimage.sa/Lessing Archive

DUFY came from a poor family but from a young age was always passionately interested in drawing, enrolling at five at the local Le Havre School of Fine Arts. Here he met Cubist pioneer and lifelong friend Georges Braque (1882–1963). Both men eventually finished their studies in Paris. In 1905 Dufy became fascinated with the color experiments of Matisse, as seen in the celebrated Salon d'Automne exhibition. He joined the Fauves, helping to develop the group's interest in geometric shapes and the decorative effects of color. By 1910 he had adopted the formal approach of Cézanne, and his work became more structured. However, this led to a severe monotone palette and the abandonment of bright colors during an unprofitable sober phase.

Dufy illustrated books for the poet Guillaume Apollinaire (1880–1918) and teamed with fashion designer Paul Poiret, creating a textile-manufacturing business. In the 1920s, he moved on to color lithography. In 1936 he was commissioned to produce the world's then largest painting for the Paris World Fair; on the theme of science and electricity, it was 70m (200ft) long. Dufy later reverted to his love of painting, resulting in the highly energetic palette seen in his Fauve-like series on casinos, regattas, and racecourses.

Fauvist

OTHON FRIESZ (1879–1949)

STILL LIFE WITH A BUDDHA

ENROLLED at the Ecole Nationale Supérieure des Beaux-Arts in 1898, along with Matisse and Rouault, Friesz drew his early influence from Impressionism but gradually adopted the distinctive and colorful style of Fauvism. He was a key member of the Fauvist Movement and his artworks were often characterized by their vibrant rhythmic shapes and stark contours. Sadly, his graphic work remains virtually unknown. This is partly due to the rarity of his early prints, which were only produced in small numbers.

Like the Impressionists, the Fauves used pure, bold colors, applied directly from their paint tubes for the fullest effect. The intention was to create emotion through color. Objects were not always depicted in their familiar tones, but as an expression of their innate qualities.

In *Still Life with a Buddha* there is a strong oriental aspect, illustrated by the Buddha in the center of the composition, the patterned vase with the drooping tulips, and the Japanese fan in the left-hand corner of the canvas. Friesz came at the tail end of the Japanese influence on Impressionism, as seen in the works of artists such as Vincent van Gogh and Claude Monet.

FRANCIS PICABIA (1879–1953)

UNDINE, OU LA DANSE

Centre Pompidou, Musée Nationale d'Art Moderne, Paris.
© DACS 2003; Francis Picabia/Celimage.sa/Lessing Archive

PARISIAN painter and renowned Cubist, Picabia was at first influenced by Matisse's Fauvism but progressed through most of the twentieth century's radical movements in art, including Futurism, Dada and Surrealism. His eclectic style oscillated constantly between figurative and abstract representation. His early Cubist work is bright and colorful, unlike the somber monotone paintings of Braque and Picasso, probably as a result of his early interest in Matisse's work. Picabia was a close friend of Marcel Duchamp (1887–1968), a pioneer in the use of ready-made art. His interest in Cubism led to a rejection of the traditional depiction of three-dimensional space, and he developed this approach in his famous series of "transparencies," which featured a series of photographic-style overlays of images to show a figure from a variety of viewpoints. After a brief flirtation with Orphism (a sub-group of Cubism), Picabia joined the European Dada movement, which made a radical bid to sabotage middle-class values through nihilism, mad lyricism, and crazy humor. He was responsible for introducing Dada to New York, where he published two Dada magazines, *291* and *391*. In common with other Dadaists, he switched his allegiance to Surrealism.

Cubist

JUAN GRIS (1887–1927)

WOMAN

Private Collection. Celimage.sa/Lessing Archive

JUAN Gris was born in Madrid, where he studied engineering before moving to Paris in 1906. He rented one of the Bateau-Lavoir studios in Montmartre, close to Picasso. Gris began his artistic career by producing drawings but was painting seriously by 1910. When Picasso's art delaer began selling Gris's works in 1911, his artistic future was confirmed.

His heavily analytical, mainly still-life Cubist works are notable for their purity and lucidity. He followed Braque and Picasso by progressing into a more accessible "synthetic" phase, in which recognizable forms were reintroduced into the world of fractured three-dimensional space. A lighter framework also meant a return to a brighter, more fluid palette, followed by the development of his monumental compositions of 1916–19. These influenced Picasso's later monolithic nude series of the early 1920s.

Gris also experimented with polychrome sculpture, inspired by Lithuanian Cubist sculptor Jacques Lipchitz (1891–1973). In his last period Gris became obsessed with color, as seen in *Woman*.

GEORGES BRAQUE (1882–1963)

STILL LIFE: THE TABLE

CUBIST pioneer Braque studied fine art in Le Havre, where he met Raoul Dufy. They moved to Paris to study, where Braque was influenced by the Fauves after witnessing their Salon d'Automne exhibition in 1905. He saw Cézanne's memorial exhibition of 1907 and incorporated these influences with elements from Picasso's groundbreaking *Les Demoiselles d'Avignon* (1907), developing them into Cubism. The term "Cubism" came from a comment made by Matisse about Braque's "little cubes." Reducing landscape and figures to somber monotone cubic shapes, Picasso and Braque brought Cubism to the limits, taking depictions of three-dimensional space and form and fracturing them into a kaleidoscope of shapes. Braque's reintroduction of lettering from newspapers and other media prevented the plunge into complete abstraction. He focused on the development of synthetic Cubism, with the inclusion of patterning, stencilling, and collage.

Seriously injured in the First World War, Braque returned to painting in 1917 and was influenced by the colorful style of his friend Juan Gris, as well as by Sergei Diaghilev's (1872–1929) Ballets Russes. By the mid-1920s, Picasso had moved into Surrealism but Braque continued with his Cubist work, as here in *Still Life: The Table*, in which he suggests three-dimensionality by exploring the different planes and facets of the objects.

Cubist

JEAN LAMBERT-RUCKI (1888-1967)

RENCONTRE

Courtesy of Edimedia

JEAN Lambert-Rucki was a painter and sculptor who participated in the artistic movements most significant at the turn of the twentieth century. He belonged to the "Artists of Montparnasse."

His works are a displacement of stylistic elements of dynamic Cubism, similar to that found in the works of Picasso and Braque. There is also an architectural aspect to his art, as seen in *Rencontre*.

However, Lambert-Rucki drew on many influences for his work. The inspiration of Africa proved to be a rich source of exotic imagery. The bold, abstract and geometric zigzags and shapes that appeared in African textiles and sculptures were adapted to suit the structure and style of Rucki's compositions. We can definitely see these elements of African art in *Rencontre*, with Rucki's use of color, circles, triangles, and zigzag forms. In this piece, we also see the African figure used as a decorative motif. In France, Lambert-Rucki and Pierre Legrain produced African-inspired sculpture, furniture, and decorative wares.

Rencontre has a blue-yellow palette, which is subtly contrasted and overlapped throughout the composition. Larger segments of sandy-brown have also been used, reinforcing the African aspect to this work.

Cubist

FERNAND LÉGER (1881–1955)

WORKERS ON SCAFFOLDING

FRENCH painter Léger began his career as an architectural designer. He was influenced by Cézanne's paintings, interpreting his Post-impressionist explorations of form as powerful and monumental blocks of color. Léger's large tubular works have a depth that is missing in the more classically Cubist approach of Picasso and Braque. He loved urban shapes and the dynamics of city life, and his work demonstrates his fascination with the dialogue between representation and abstraction to redefine three-dimensional space. During the First World War he began painting working men and machinery, intrinsic themes in much of his subsequent work. Consequently, he was allied to the Italian Futurist movement but was one of the first to progress into complete abstraction. Although touched by Surrealism, Léger maintained a rationalist approach after coming into contact with the Purism movement of Le Corbusier (1887–1965) in the 1920s. *Workers on Scaffolding*, one of his later works, shows his preoccupation with capturing objects and figures in "free space," the tubular solidity of the men and materials contrasting with the backdrop of the open sky.

Cubist

BALLA, who had no academic training, set up as a painter in Turin, where he worked until 1895. Moving to Rome, he worked on portraits, landscapes, and scenes of the Roman streets, while keeping up with Neo-impressionist developments in Paris. He methodically explored the representation of light in paint.

Balla had worked with two much younger painters, Umberto Boccioni and Gino Severini. In 1909 Boccioni composed his two futurist manifestos and Balla became one of the first signatories. The futurist "discovery" that the space through which bodies move is never straight but is curved, or even circular, chimed with his own growing rejection of the static universe, and resembled Einstein's special theory of relativity which, with its demonstration that space-time is indeed curved, was published in 1905.

Balla now turned out canvases whose effect resembled that of movement when photographed at a slow shutter speed. He also became interested in the attempts by some futurists to produce a visual equivalent of noise. This is the subject of the painting illustrated. The sequence of the title words is significant: two abstract words and then the clinching concrete signifier: motorcyclist. Balla's design achieves its effect by exploiting the wheels of the machine, its tires, cogs, and flying chain, unraveling them and feeding them into a vortex, while fire or electricity sparks between them. The reverberant quality of noise is also there, as Balla's various moving coils echo each other. This is abstraction of a kind that, though it owed much to Cubism, had not previously been seen in painting.

PAUL KLEE (1879–1940)

THE NECKLACE

Das Halsband, 1932, 227 (V7), 22.6 x 32.2cm, watercolor on paper,
Schenkung LK, Klee-Museum, Bern. Celimage.sa/Lessing Archive

KLEE was certainly an exception to many of his contemporaries. His work does not strictly coincide with any recognizable progression of artistic ideals of the time, but rather mirrors his own personal philosophy and conveys an inner meaning, which is sometimes more important than the content of the painting itself. Klee often kept his canvases quite small so that his messages were not lost amidst them.

The Necklace (1932) is an interesting blend of neutral watercolor used in a unique and distinctive manner, held loosely on the paper canvas. Klee tended to see the world as a model, run by the cosmic clockmaker, a Swiss God, who was supposed to embody spiritual truth. His philosophy was translated into his artwork, and he presents the figures in his paintings in a toy-like way, to mirror his fantasies. Like Kandinsky, Klee marveled at the art of children. He envied their innocence and directness and recreated them in his works. In *The Necklace*, we can see how Klee applies his paint in a free, childlike fashion, not watching for detailed outlines, but merely applying his medium to weakly resemble the objects or people he paints. The blotted and overlapping effect of his technique gives *The Necklace* a unique artistic perspective, and one that is personal to Klee. The picture looks as though it is still moving as the paint blurs around the edges of the faces, which are set in contrast to the sharp and delicately painted eyes and necklace. These provide a focal point to the painting, which might otherwise not be recognizable for what it is.

NAUM GABO (1890–1977)

LINEAR CONSTRUCTION NO. 4

Tate Gallery, London © DACS 2003; Naum Gabo/Courtesy of Edimedia

RUSSIAN-BORN sculptor Gabo trained initially as an engineer in Munich. He worked alongside his artist brother, Antoine Pevsner (1886–1962), who kept the family name, and both were heavily influenced by the Cubists. On returning to Moscow, they became involved with the avant-garde post-revolutionary Proletariat art movement led by Kasimir Malevich (1878–1935), Vladimir Tatlin (1885–1953), and Kandinsky (1866–1944). The brothers wrote the influential *Realistic Manifesto* (1920), which renounced the idea of static mass as the basis for art and expounded the notions of "rhythm" and movement in abstract work as the basis of kinetic art. When the Constructivist movement was split by an ideological battle between functionalism and more spiritual objectives, the brothers were forced into exile with Kandinsky and Moholy-Nagy. They first went to Berlin and then to Paris. Gabo eventually moved to Britain, where he was highly influential on the work of Barbara Hepworth (1903–75) and Ben Nicholson (1894–1982). He then joined Moholy-Nagy's re-formed Bauhaus group in the US, where he lived from 1939. Working in glass, plastic, and metal, Gabo influenced Moholy-Nagy's Bauhaus work, using light materials to show sculpture's non-static interaction with modular space. Movement and a sense of weightlessness were implied through light falling on geometric structures, as seen here in the dynamic *Linear Construction No. 4*, made from aluminum and stainless steel.

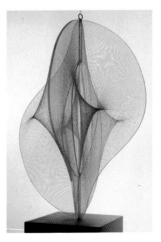

GIORGIO DE CHIRICO (1888–1978)

PIAZZA D'ITALIA

ITALIAN painter de Chirico is lauded as the precursor of one of the most influential and far-reaching art movements of the twentieth century: Surrealism. He was born in Greece and later studied in Athens, Florence, and Munich. De Chirico was deeply affected by the Symbolist paintings of Böcklin (1827–1901), admiring their blend of the surreal with the real. In 1917 he met Carlo Carrà (1881–1966) while recovering from a breakdown, and together they founded the Metaphysical movement.

Although the movement was short-lived, de Chirico's Metaphysical paintings mark the height of his career. They were hugely influential on Surrealist artists, who recognized in them the eloquent expression of the unconscious and nonsensical to which they themselves aspired. By the 1920s, however, de Chirico had moved to a more conventional form of expression. The Surrealists, in particular, condemned his later work, which never attained the level of success of his Metaphysical work.

The apparently random inclusion of objects in *Piazza d'Italia* is typical of de Chirico's Metaphysical paintings. The Italian architecture was a familiar motif, as was the distant train. A sense of emptiness and vast space is apparent, and despite the inclusion of the two figures this appears a solitary, forgotten place.

Surrealist

MARCEL DUCHAMP (1887–1968)

NUDE DESCENDING THE STAIRCASE

Philadelphia Museum of Art © DACS 2003; Marcel Duchamp

MARCEL Duchamp was a leading painter, sculptor, and art theorist. He was a key initiator of the Dada Movement and a leading spirit within the Avant-garde artists, during first decades of the twentieth century. The Impressionist painter Paul Cézanne influenced Duchamp initially, although he was subsequently inspired by the Fauvist Movement, especially in the contextual use of color. *In Nude Descending the Staircase* we can see that the artist employed similar techniques and compositional styles to the Italian Futurists. There are particularly strong parallels with Giacomo Balla (1871–1958) and Umberto Boccioni (1882–1916).

In this painting the artist depicts the successive movements of a single figure. There is a riot of action as the subject moves downward through several apparent cycles of motion. There is a comparison to be drawn with the shapes of people in the figurative paintings of Giorgio de Chirico (1888–1978). Duchamp succeeds in transforming Cubist elements into a Futurist cum Dadaist conflation. The Dada movement was a direct precursor of the Surrealists, and Duchamp, whose later sculptural works included urinals as well as household objects, can be seen as a key figure in that evolution.

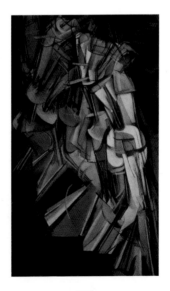

GEORGIA O'KEEFFE (1887–1986)

YELLOW CALLA

PERHAPS the most prominent of modern female artists, O'Keeffe was born in Wisconsin, studying art in Chicago and New York before working as a commercial artist in Chicago. By 1912 O'Keeffe had become an art teacher. While teaching, O'Keeffe began to develop her notoriously unique style and by 1915 was producing stylized, almost abstract images. Without her knowledge, a friend showed her work to photographer and art dealer Alfred Stieglitz (1864–1946), who included it in an exhibition in New York. The pictures were a success and in 1917 Stieglitz put on O'Keeffe's first one-woman show.

Following an illness, O'Keeffe moved to New York, accepting sponsorship from Alfred Stieglitz so that she could stop teaching to concentrate more fully on her art. O'Keeffe and Stieglitz married in 1923; his photographic work was a stimulus for her famous paintings of skyscrapers and enlarged close-ups of flowers.

Georgia O'Keeffe captured the sensuality and allure of flowers in the flowing curves of her extraordinary paintings. During the second half of the nineteenth century, the exotic South African calla lily was introduced in the United States, and it began to appear as a subject in American art. The flower became more popular with artists after Sigmund Freud offered a sexual interpretation of its form. From the 1920s, the calla lily became a recurring motif in Georgia O'Keeffe's work.

Surrealist

HANS BELLMER (1902–75)

CEPHALOPOD

IN 1934, the erotic imagination of the German–Polish, then French artist, Hans Bellmer, was publicly displayed in the Surrealist journal *Minotaure*. Photographs of a life-size, female doll laid bare the complex and fraught mind of the artist.

Bellmer's known interest in young girls as subjects for his art is explored again in *Cephalopod*. Here there is displayed a raw sexuality that denies the femininity of the subject, the focal point being the bodily orifice exposed through distorted, contorted limbs. There is absolutely no restraint, subtlety, or sensitivity in this harsh work. The face wears an expression of disinterested resignation. Bellmer offers no insight into the subject, but instead overwhelms us through his angry, violent impulses.

Cephalopod is an illustration of Bellmer's warped perception of the female form and hints darkly at the domineering perspective on the young female. There is total anatomical distortion, with legs, but no arms, a twisted torso, and a skewered head. The overall effect is violent and provocative.

Perhaps this type of work is what André Breton had in mind when he coined the term "convulsive beauty" to describe the works of art that he most admired.

KURT SCHWITTERS (1887–1948)

PICTURE WITH BASKET RING

SCHWITTERS was close friends with many German Dadaists, despite the fact that he disagreed with some of their views. What he admired was their love of nonsense; what he defended was the value and importance of art over politics. He did not want to generate a revolution, but rather to construct a better world. He worked with society's discarded objects, building them into sublime examples of human creativity.

The history of collage is dominated by Schwitters, although other Dadaists and Surrealists experimented with this medium, and Georges Braque and Umberto Boccioni were to become early exponents of the art form. Pablo Picasso, Jean Dubuffet, and even Henri Mattisse produced widely varying collage works. In Schwitters excellence was reached. He utilized everyday as well as cast-off objects and materials.

The objects in this collage recall an urban geometry and excitement, and a more curved line begins to appear. The rounded shape heralds a move toward more natural materials and a collage method that was becoming deeper and more sculptural—an assemblage of objects rather than a collage made of flat paper.

SIR HENRY MOORE (1898–1986)

FAMILY GROUP

Henry Moore Foundation, Much Hadham. Celimage.sa/Lessing Archive

HENRY Moore was one of the most highly esteemed and influential British modern artists, his innovative work pushing British art toward modernism. Born in Yorkshire, Moore knew at the age of ten that he wanted to create sculptures. In 1919, following military service, Moore received a grant to study art in Leeds and in 1921 he studied at London's Royal College of Art. While British sculpture was still conventionally representational, Moore became increasingly drawn to primitive art (especially Mexican), with its greater spontaneity and freedom of form.

In the 1930s Moore's work took on Surrealist tones; while visiting Paris, Moore had admired the works of Arp (1887–1966), Miró (1893–1983), and particularly Picasso (1881–1973). It was during this "Surrealist" period that Moore first sculpted a human figure formed from several separate pieces, as in *Reclining Figure.*

In *Family Group* the figures are presented as accentuated, almost surreal forms. Their curves and sizes are enhanced, so that the figures are merely suggested rather than realistically portrayed. The theme of the human form had great fascination for Moore, and he returned to it frequently. His sculptures evoke the potential beauty and energy of the human form.

RENÉ MAGRITTE (1898–1967)

THE EMPIRE OF LIGHT II

BELGIAN Surrealistic painter René Magritte, along with artists such as James Ensor and André Delvaux, was one of the most significant artists of the twentieth century and, specifically, the Surrealist movement. He created a substantial number of artworks, including over 1,100 paintings and 700 gouaches, as well as designing posters and illustrating numerous scores. *The Empire of Light II* also inspired several re-creations and variations of the painting by artists such as Johan de Meij.

Typically of the Surrealists painters, and Magritte himself, *The Empire of Light* upsets and distorts our normal perception of the environment, forcing us to reconsider what we accept as "normal." This painting is particularly disturbing because of its paradoxical portrayal of day and night. A pitch-black street and house, dimly lit by a street lamp, are set in deep contrast to a brightly colored, cloud-dotted blue sky. The bright sky is so distracting that we are unable to decipher the features of the house.

The painting itself creates an eerie and haunting feel, caused by Magritte's photographic regeneration of an everyday scene. This makes his distortion of day and night so much more profound, as it seems so real. Again, Magritte successfully manages to convey something that is both surreal and aesthetically admirable.

Surrealist

YVES TANGUY (1900–55)

MULTIPLICATION OF THE ARCS

YVES Tanguy is one of the more neglected Surrealists. As far back as 1982, a retrospective in Baden-Baden was the last exhibition dedicated to his works, despite the fact that he was part of the inner circle of the Surrealist group.

Allegedly, after having visited a de Chirico exhibition at the Galérie Paul Guillaume in Paris, Tanguy spontaneously decided to become a painter. However, the influence of de Chirico's work is now considered to have lasted only until 1923–24, when Tanguy branched out to draw and paint in watercolors, and then became influenced by Dadaism. This debate continues, since subtle elements of color or distortion can still be detected in Tanguy's artworks, similar to those of de Chirico, as late as 1942.

The intention of Tanguy's artworks and their titles was to confuse and provoke the viewer. His works mapped the artist's search for the "reality in the unconscious," and for dreams. *Multiplication of the Arcs* is a clear example of this exploration. It is dominated by a dreary sky. Black shadows provide a contrast with the multiplicity of beings, while the white partitions blocking their path represent the black and white poles.

In *Multiplication of the Arcs* Tanguy demonstrates an astonishingly accomplished technicality. The foreground of his canvas is completely filled with an intricacy of shell-like beings that beckon to an abrupt and darkly cast horizon.

JOAN MIRÓ (1893–1983)

STUDY FOR A MONUMENT OFFERED TO THE CITY OF BARCELONA

Matisse Collection, New York © DACS 2003; Joan Miró/
Celimage.sa/Scala Archives

THE Spanish painter Miró was the son of a rich goldsmith. He originally thought of studying business but eventually chose art instead, studying in his home town of Barcelona. While living in Paris, Miró became involved with the Dada movement, before joining the Surrealists in 1924. Experimental to the last, in his late career Miró explored the fields of ceramics and stained glass.

Miró probably came the closest to achieving the Surrealist goal: using chance and the unconscious as methods of exploring the "unreal." In much of his work, Miró employed a technique approaching automatism and his paintings are filled with psychologically pertinent symbols, amid randomly defined forms. There is often an incoherence in his work, stemming from his distorted, primary images, and leaning toward Abstract Expressionism.

This delightful sculpture, housed at the Matisse Collection in New York, offers an enchanting example of Surrealist sculpture. It is a study or trial model for a work to celebrate the Catalan capital. We can see the striking metallic form of an abstract sculptor. We are presented with a cold, thrusting shape that is devoid of the painter's usual bright colors.

215

SALVADOR DALÍ (1904–89)

THE LAST SUPPER

THE Last Supper is an outstanding and painterly work on an epic scale. In later life Dalí was to work increasingly on large-scale paintings and frescoes. The strongly religious theme of this work reflects his lifelong adherence to strong Catholic beliefs. This work is set to stand amongst the greatest religious paintings of all time. The Last Supper is a much-treated theme from the early Renaissance to the Baroque, but never before did a painter create such a highly reverential yet deeply unorthodox view of this scene from the last days of the life of Christ.

The painting is quite simply flowing with symbolism. Jesus signals toward an image of himself crucified. The disciples are truly overwhelmed by the ominous gravity of Christ's presence. Dalí manages to convey the man Jesus in transition to eternal iconic status as the Christ rising, through death, to heaven.

The supremely balanced interweaving of the geometric framework of windows offers a modern parameter to a biblical scene. The soft, glowing sky lends power and supreme majesty to the setting.

The table is adorned with a photo-realistic cloth, which drapes to the floor. In the distance, we see the calm waters extend to distant hills. This is a moving and inspirational tour de force. The artist is indeed the master of all he has created. Dalí, above all other twentieth-century artists, combined superhuman technical ability with a vivid, almost limitless imagination.

Surrealist

PABLO PICASSO (1881–1973)

GUERNICA

BORN in Spain, Picasso was undoubtedly the twentieth century's master of form. He dictated the direction of art for the first 50 years of the century and worked prolifically until his death at the age of 92.

Following his revolutionary painting *Les Demoiselles d'Avignon* (1907), he founded Cubism with Georges Braque (1882–1963), then went on to pioneer Dada and Surrealism. In later years he experimented with unique ways of seeing the world, often painting the women in his life, but never fully descended into abstraction. He lived in France, occasionally returning to Spain until the savagery of the Spanish Civil War, during which he produced this painting, his most famous work.

A powerful political statement, it was a reaction to the Fascist bombing of the Basque town of Guernica. The monumental 26-ft mural represented art's condemnation of Fascism. The painting pivots around the central pyramidal structure, balanced by curves and straight lines. Picasso discarded color to intensify the drama, producing a reportage-like photographic record. Appalling images of mutilation, death, and destruction, which Picasso had explored in earlier mythological bull scenes, reach an anguished crescendo.

Surrealist

MAN RAY (1890–1977)

CADEAU. REPLICA OF 1921 ORIGINAL

CLOSELY affiliated to the Surrealist artist Marcel Duchamp for over 50 years, Man Ray produced a number of readymades, assisted ready-mades, and various compositions, which often incorporated a more complex undertone. They were purposefully created to satirize, annoy, confuse, shock, and evoke a reaction.

The one thing Man Ray's readymades were not intended to do, was create an aesthetic presence, rather they placed an everyday object in an unusual context or position, and thus, made it art. In his sculpture *Cadeau*, Man Ray uses an everyday object, an iron, which is produced from cast iron, with the obvious difference that sharp spikes protrude from its surface. It is a simply formed sculpture, which requests the observer to question their pre-established perception of the object in a novel way, and reflect upon it. However, the original of *Cadeau* was lost, and this is a re-creation.

Man Ray continued to create such artworks throughout his long career, always managing to venture beyond the consensus, leading the way into the avant-garde. This meant that the artist delved into every conceivable medium, leading to his long-established status as an artist who set a precedent for his successors.

MAX ERNST (1891–1976)

THE FOREST

THE Forest is one of several such paintings that Ernst completed in his lifetime. The forest theme continued into his later works, such as *Lovers in the Forest* (1957) and *The Last Forest* (1960), a revolt against nature's forces of growth.

This series of paintings illustrates Ernst's further experiments into artistic techniques such as frottage, etching, and grating. In *The Forest*, he uses frottage for the trunks of the trees. This is a unique technique, which offers a graphic and realistic edge to his works.

This innovative streak stemmed from André Breton's Surrealist Manifesto of 1924, in which he encouraged artists to work with an element of chance in their paintings, and in the way in which they used their materials. Ernst was certainly influenced by these ideas, which led to the development of techniques that can be seen throughout his later works.

In *The Forest*, it seems as though the figures are constructed out of the leaves and bark that surround them. Their arms are extended above their heads, which are tilted upward, as though in desperation, or perhaps out of joy. Their bodies, outlined in white, stand out against the dark background, complementing the gradient of the lines of the trees.

ANDRÉ MASSON (1896–1987)

BATTLE OF FISHES

DURING the First World War, the French painter André Masson was badly injured. In the aftermath of this he redirected his energies toward a new revolutionary stance, and he joined the Surrealist movement, viewing it as the only artistic movement worth being associated with, because of its liberation from tradition. Although he would later dissociate himself from the movement, Masson was truly liberated as an artist through Surrealism. His work became far more experimental and spontaneous than precise, and he began using a variety of media.

Battle of Fishes was one of Masson's early Surrealist works. In this artwork, we can see Masson experimenting with texture by throwing sand onto a canvas covered with glue. He has used sand, gesso, oil, pencil, and charcoal on his canvas. We can see how his use of color has also become more creative, with sections of red paint being contrasted against a deep, murky green. This emphasizes a certain tension in the artwork, as areas of bright color are set in juxtaposition to Masson's single pencil lines and a neutral-colored background, which is itself texturally contrasted with his generous use of sand.

Surrealist

FRIDA KAHLO (1907–54)

FULANG-CHANG AND I

KAHLO'S renown and popularity have grown partly because of the intensely autobiographical content of her work, which reflects the intriguing details of her short life. In 1925 Kahlo was left disabled and infertile following a traffic accident; she had planned a career in medicine but this became impossible. Wracked with pain, Kahlo began painting during her recovery. In 1928 she married fellow Mexican Diego Rivera (1886–1957), a prominent painter. Their relationship was stormy with affairs, divorce, and remarriage following in later years (most famously Kahlo had an affair with Trotsky, who was later murdered in her house).

Kahlo did not have formal art training and her style of painting is influenced by Mexican folk art, so her work is termed "naive." Although often associated with the Surrealists, because of the highly symbolic, hallucinatory quality of her paintings, she did not view herself as one.

Kahlo's paintings of herself with her pet monkeys were very popular. She often painted ribbons that connected herself to objects or other people.

ALBERTO GIACOMETTI (1901–66)

SIX BRONZE FIGURES

GIACOMETTI produced 90 sculptures, 40 paintings, and 60 drawings in his lifetime. Many of his artworks, such as his sculpture, employed a wide range of themes and techniques. For example, *Spoon Woman* (1926–27), celebrates women and sexuality, but in an abstract form, incorporating a blend of influence from African art and Cubism. Although he is generally associated with the Surrealist movement, Giacometti has been called an Existentialist, an Abstract Expressionist, and even a Cubist. His bronze figures have contributed to his reputation as one of the most outstanding sculptors of the twentieth century.

This particular collection has a deeper and darker connotation. The figures, lined as they are in a straight row, remind us of the survivors of the concentration camps of the Second World War. They appear collectively frail and emaciated in form, and seem slightly unbalanced on their bases, as though they are weightless. Looking closely toward the feet and supports of the figures, they appear to have collected a film of brown dust, which adds to their overall warlike and apocalyptic impression. Although featureless, the varying heights of the figures provide them with an element of individuality, as each one has been crafted slightly differently. Positioned outside, these figures all catch the light slightly differently, creating an individual, but slightly unnerving presence.

JEAN ARP (1887–1966)

WOMAN

FRENCH artist Jean Arp is associated with several modern art movements. In 1911 he took part in the Blue Rider exhibitions in Munich, with Kandinsky (1866–1944). The Cubist art he saw in Paris in 1914 also greatly impressed him. His quintessential artistic belief was the concept of the creativity of a freed unconscious mind; freedom was to be found in primary, basic, spontaneous art forms. Arp was also a poet and attempted automatism (involuntary or unconscious action) in the creative process.

On the outbreak of the First World War, Jean Arp traveled to Switzerland, settling in Zurich with his future wife, artist Sophie Taeuber (1889–1943). They were both involved in the emerging Dada movement in Zurich, attending infamous "happenings" at the Cabaret Voltaire. By 1925 Arp had moved to a town near Paris and took part in the first Surrealist exhibition. Although he retained his independence, he was closely linked with the Surrealists thereafter.

By the 1930s Arp moved away from his earlier collages, making sculptures "in the round." Like his collages, the sculptures are simple abstract forms made from natural substances. The contours of his sculptures, such as *Woman*, flow freely, suggestive of forms found in nature. Arp's sculptures impressed the Surrealists, especially Joan Miró, and his influence is also evident in the work of Henry Moore.

WASSILY KANDINSKY (1866–1944)

LANDSCAPE

KANDINSKY is seen as the father of abstract art. He was born in Moscow, and trained as a lawyer before turning to art at the age of 30. He discovered the Symbolists' interest in the occult after meeting the French Nabis and Fauvist groups during a stay in Paris, when he exhibited at the Salon of 1906.

Kandinsky became increasingly concerned with color and reductionism of form, and briefly joined the German Expressionist group Die Brücke (The Bridge), who were experimenting with the linear rhythmical expression that was to become his hallmark in abstraction. The first abstract appeared in 1910.

Landscape (1913) is a hypnotic mixture of colors, which spiral between a mixture of line and shape. The group of avant-garde artists that included Picasso, Braque, Delaunay, and Klee, were interested in the psychological power of line and color, as applied in a primitive and childlike way, but containing an inherent symbolism. Their works captured drama and movement, pulsating with the energy of their explosive color.

Abstract Expressionist

224

PIET MONDRIAN (1872–1944)

COMPOSITION IN BLUE, YELLOW, AND WHITE

Künsthalle, Basel. © DACS 2003; Piet Mondrian/Celimage.sa/Scala Archives

MONDRIAN was brought up in a strict Calvinist Dutch family. His father and uncle were both painters. He developed his own spiritual-science philosophy of asceticism into a powerful new art form, which he called Neoplasticism, in which shapes, lines, and colors all have autonomous values and relationships. Using these principles, he attempted to create paintings of harmony based on an expressionless sense of order.

He studied initially at the Amsterdam Academy but a move to Paris in 1909 introduced him to Cubism. This resulted in his wonderful egg series (*Pier and Ocean*, 1914), in which a field of crosses creates a unity of shape, based on theosophy's symbolic belief in the egg as a signifier of the birth of the universe.

Back in Holland in 1914, he developed the *Compositions* series, in which flat rectangles of primary colors are set in a distinctive black grid. Reducing form to strict geometric shapes, he moved colors around the framework until they "felt right." A sense of action in apparent stillness is created within the confines of each section of the painting; the white-framed squares seem to leap out. Mondrian formulated the De Stijl movement in 1917, which influenced Bauhaus. On the outbreak of the Second World War, he joined Naum Gabo (1890–1977) in London, before moving permanently to New York in 1940.

CONSTANTIN BRANCUSI (1876–1957)

THE KISS

PLACED alongside Picasso (1881–1973) as one of the twentieth century's major sculptors, Romanian-born Constantin Brancusi first trained as a carpenter and stonemason before studying sculpture in Bucharest. He moved to Paris in 1904, working briefly for Rodin (1840–1917). Fascinated like Picasso by African and primitive art, he was involved, along with Piet Mondrian (1872–1944), in the beliefs of theosophy, which led him to Hindu, Buddhist, and oriental art. This saw him radically simplifying images into universal symbols of life and fertility, although he never resorted to purely geometrical works like Mondrian's. Brancusi's strength is in simplification, as here in *The Kiss*, which was seen as a sculptural counterpart to Picasso's ground-breaking *Les Demoiselles d'Avignon* (1907) in its reduction of form.

Brancusi's sculpture heralded minimalism and affected the development of abstract art. Another celebrated piece, *Endless Column* (1920), was seen as a turning point in sculpture with its emphasis on beautifully symmetrical carving and a love of material. As British sculptor Henry Moore (1898–1987) declared, "he made us shape-conscious." Although he worked until his death at the age of 81, he produced only 220 works, which in later years he was reluctant to part with, simply polishing their surfaces.

Abstract Expressionist

ARSHILE GORKY (1905–48)

GARDEN IN SOCHI

USE of primary color and fine line suggest a certain naivety, but also gives a refined power to the artwork. Its grain effect gives the color texture, and the vibrancy of the yellow, in particular, imparts a wild, erratic quality. With the loose, almost sketchy application of the medium, which leaves areas of shape unfilled, Gorky creates a raw quality and a sense of motion and incompleteness to the whole image. As with the drip-drying technique used in *The Leaf of the Artichoke is an Owl*, Gorky makes us believe that perhaps he intended more for the image. In some areas, the color has been applied quite thinly, to create a watery effect. This is particularly evident toward the left-hand side of the canvas. Gorky also used this technique in *The Waterfall*, (c. 1943), in order to recreate the naturalistic qualities of his observations. However, in terms of his use of color, *Garden in Sochi* is limited in its palette, whereas in *The Waterfall* and *Year After Year* (1947), he takes a far more liberal approach. The blank canvas in *Garden in Sochi* gives a sense of bleakness to the image, in contrast with his usual color-consumed paintings.

Gorky took his early influences from Picasso, before joining the Surrealists in the mid-1920s. He went on to become a significant and influential member of the Surrealist movement. His works can be seen at New York's Guggenheim and Whitney Museums.

Abstract Expressionist

JACKSON POLLOCK (1912–56)

NUMBER 12

WHEN most people think of Abstract Expressionism, they think of Pollock. As Willem de Kooning said, "Pollock broke the ice." Born in Wyoming, he eventually drifted to New York where he studied art, and also painted vast murals on public buildings as part of the WPA (Works Progress Administration) government employment project during the Depression. He was one of the few American members of the non-geometric New York Abstract Expressionist art group of mainly European exiles, but shared their experience of dislocation to an alien city. He absorbed influences from Picasso, Mondrian, and Miró, and became associated with American Surrealism, contributing to the 1942 International Surrealist Exhibition.

The Abstract Expressionists' concern with mythology led to his first "drip painting" in 1947, in which form is initially non-specific but resolves itself during execution. Pollock believed that "painting has life of its own, which I let come through" and often stood in the middle of his canvases to work, enjoying being a physical part of the "action painting" process. As he laid down acres of paint, often with found objects such as cigarettes and buttons embedded in it, haunting structural forms emerged from the chaotic mass, as in *Number 12*. Pollock died in a car accident in 1956.

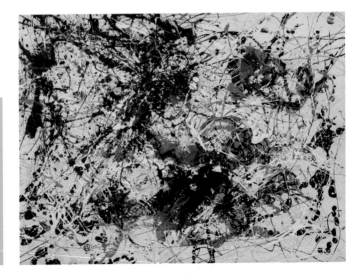

Abstract Expressionist

WILLEM DE KOONING (1904–97)

THE WAVE

THE early career of this Dutch artist was influenced by Piet Mondrian's De Stijl movement. In 1926 he moved to the US, where he, like Pollock, became a decorator in the WPA arts project set up by government to organize employment during the Depression. The project employed 5,000 artists who concentrated on public service works such as the monumental murals by de Kooning and Gorky (1905–48).

In the 1940s de Kooning became a leading member of the New York Abstract Expressionists, a group of mainly European exiles based in New York's Greenwich Village. Their pioneering "action art" took abstract developments into new fields, and the effects are still apparent today. Eventually the group split into two factions: one characterized by the textural brush painting of Pollock and de Kooning, the other centered on the color-field work of Barnett Newman (1905–70) and Mark Rothko (1903–70). The struggle between the forces of nature, a drama of land and sea is mapped across *The Wave*, where a lavish fusion of marine and earth colors struggles for attention. Momentum and force are bound together in this powerful work.

Abstract Expressionist

229

MARK ROTHKO (1903–70)

WITHOUT TITLE (SOMETIMES KNOWN AS DARK BLUE ON A DARK BLUE BACKGROUND)

AT the age of ten, Russian-born Rothko emigrated with his family to the US. He dropped out of Yale University to take up art. In common with other members of the Abstract Expressionist group, during the Depression he worked on the WPA arts project before establishing a New York art school, "Subjects of the Artist," in 1948 with Barnett Newman (1905–70). Inspired by Joan Miró and Surrealism, Rothko progressed into Abstract Expressionism.

Eventually Newman and Rothko formed a splinter group that concentrated on unified color-field work that differed from the textured brush painting of Pollock and de Kooning. Rothko was particularly significant for his development of the abstract forms of luminous color that hover like blurred horizontal mists against dramatic colored backgrounds, as seen in *Dark Blue on a Dark Blue Background*. Such work led to critical aesthetic debate on whether the use of one color could constitute art. Rothko believed that such paintings represented "clarity, elimination of all obstacles between the painter and idea, and idea and observer." Influenced by Turner's sunsets, he wanted his work to induce deep contemplation of a color plane, which he hoped would bring the viewer in touch with their basic human emotions. The darkening palette of the late 1950s heralded Rothko's decline into depression, which led to his suicide in 1970.

Abstract Expressionist

BARNETT NEWMAN (1905–70)

VIR HEROICUS SUBLIMIS

BORN in New York to Jewish immigrants, Barnett Newman worked in his father's clothing factory for a while before taking up painting full time and becoming a founder member of the Abstract Expressionist movement. He gave up painting for a while in the 1940s to write art theories and establish a New York art school, "Subjects of the Artist," with Mark Rothko.

He returned to painting, and as an existentialist he believed art's duty was to express the terror that sprang from tragedy—he was deeply affected by the effects of the atom bombs on Hiroshima and Nagasaki at the end of the Second World War. He often used mythological and biblical themes to evoke spirituality in his paintings, and his subject matter was the "terrible self," which centered on personal awareness rather than the subconscious world of Surrealism. His work prompted critical debate on the nature of art; like Rothko, he believed that contemplation of color created emotional and spiritual effects in the viewer. *Vir Heroicus Sublimis* is a typical example of his vast, single-color fields, which were often red and split by "zips," or bands, as a device to open up the picture plane. The elegant *Onement* (1946) initiated this series.

Newman also produced large steel sculptures, in which he developed the use of a single line in space to signify the universal chain of life.

Abstract Expressionist

JASPER JOHNS (1930–)

MAP

BORN in South Carolina, Johns studied at the Carolina State University, arriving in New York in 1952, where he fell under the spell of the Abstract Expressionists. His work is now seen as the critical link between Abstract Expressionism and the emerging Post-modernist and Pop Art movement, with its love of ironies, paradox, and parody. Johns was influenced by Marcel Duchamp's (1887–1968) pioneering work in this field.

The choice of mundane subject matter, such as targets, numbers, and the famous *American Flag* series, is a feature of Post-modernist irony. Perhaps even more ironic is the fact that Johns's *White Flag* (1958), now in the New York Metropolitan Museum, is valued at more than $20 million.

Johns concentrated on abstract qualities of texture, color, and drawing within a representational environment, as seen in this painting, *Map*. His style, with exaggerated strokes and use of repetition, underlines his concern for techniques. In later work he started to combine surface collage and sculpture, as in *Field Painting* (1963–64), in which he adapted Barnett Newman's "zip" line to include old slogans, advertising, and mass media items such as coffee tins and beer cans. Such work helped to inspire Andy Warhol's (1928–87) later Campbell's soup pieces.

FRANK STELLA (1936–)

KASTURA

BORN in 1936 in Massachusetts, Stella studied painting at the Phillips Academy, MA, also graduating in history from Princeton. He arrived in New York in 1959 and began to explore the new expressions of formal abstraction, developing Jasper Johns's use of repetition and flat color.

Pioneering early Minimalism, the young Stella strove to isolate pictorial space from that of the real world. He purged art of all metaphor and meaning, and coined the term "non-relational" to refer to this style (it is also known as post-painterly abstraction and hard-edge painting). His early work in the 1950s tested the purity of abstraction in a controversial series of monochrome black paintings, which emphasized symmetry and the flatness of the canvas.

Later Stella progressed to "systemic abstraction," concentrating on repetition or progression of a single element in monumental U- and L-shaped canvases. In the late 1960s he turned to brilliantly colored semicircles—the "Protractor" series, of which *Kastura* is an example—forcing the viewer to focus on the object rather than some external reality. This led to mixed-media reliefs and metal works, in which Stella challenged the boundaries between painting and sculpture. The sculpture-paintings produced in the 1980s are an exuberant combination of forms and patterning.

Post-modernist

JOSEPH BEUYS (1921–86)

EURASIAN SIBERIAN SYMPHONY

BEUYS was Germany's most important post-war artist. The breadth of his vision spanned installation, video, and performance art. He joined the German airforce during the Second World War, and after his plane crashed on the Russian steppes his life was saved by Tartar tribespeople, who covered him in fat to keep him warm. This incident later had a profound effect on his artistic output.

He studied art in Düsseldorf between 1946–51, when he became cathartically obsessed with images of wounding, the Cross, and Madonna and Child, eventually turning to massive sculptures in fat and wax. *Tallow* and *Queen Bee* serve as emblems of his own spiritual healing. Beuys pioneered installation art, developing his 'social sculpture' theories by incorporating mundane objects into exhibits. This dislocation of ordinary objects was innovative in the developing Post-modernist climate and influenced many subsequent artists working in installation art.

Beuys often created a score or "partita" (as opposed to a script) in which he would plan the objects that would be used in the sequence of the performance. He saw each action as a new version of a basic theme and an attempt to make his philosophy more comprehensible.

DONALD JUDD (1928–94)

UNTITLED (STACK)

BORN in Missouri, Judd was a veteran of the Korean War who began painting at the Art Students' League before completing his studies in postgraduate art history at Columbia. Dissatisfied with painting and Abstract Expressionism, he pioneered Minimalism in the early 1960s with his reliefs and freestanding structures. Judd sought to remove the artist from the creative equation and, like Stella, strove to isolate pictorial space from that of the real world. His views paved the way for conceptual art and his radical simplicity affected the Minimalist design movement. He disliked the word Minimalism and refused to call his work "sculpture," believing that the term implied carving. Judd's smooth cubic and rectangular works redefined post-war sculpture, eliminating pedestals and stressing open, weightless mass. The structures were often in beautiful metals, as in this *Untitled (Stack)* from 1972, or translucent plexiglass. The pieces were machine-made by other people to avoid the artist's hand, recalling László Moholy-Nagy's Bauhaus kinetic constructions. Judd insisted on perfection: mathematical precision was of primary importance.

FRIEDRICH HUNDERTWASSER (1928–2000)

"HUNDERTWASSER-HOUSE" IN KEGELGASSE, VIENNA

FRIEDENSREICH Hundertwasser was born on December 15 1928 in Vienna. He is now considered to be one of the leading artists to emerge on the international art scene since the Second World War, producing a large number of paintings and graphics.

He produced this apartment house with "tree tenants" in the windows and on the balconies. He used different colors to delineate the size of individual apartments. From this particular photograph, we are viewing the apartments directly in front of us. They appear as a mosaic of color, which, in the bright sunlight, becomes luminous. The vibrant jigsaw quality of the colors of the building, and the loose lines within which they are fitted, remind us of the buildings by the Spanish architect, Antonio Gaudí.

Hundertwasser is attempting to offer us a paradise through his works, using them to give voice to ideas that society has found questionable, particularly his views on religion and the human condition.

Post-modernist

RICHARD HAMILTON (1922–)

PIN UP

LONDON-BORN Hamilton is seen as the father of Pop Art and a major influence on subsequent devotees, including Andy Warhol (1928–87). His art education at the Royal Academy in London was interrupted by the Second World War, during which he retrained as an engineering draftsman. An academic, he taught at the Central School of Arts and Crafts in London, and then at Newcastle University. He helped to establish the late-1950s Independent Group, whose members included artists, critics, and architects. It met in London at the Institute of Contemporary Arts (ICA) to discuss and popularize mass US culture.

Pop Art borrowed materials and techniques from other media, such as airbrushing and silk-screen effects, in a vast celebration of popular culture and the effects of the global mass media. Subsequently there was a creation of new universal icons, from household advertising names to superstars like Marilyn Monroe.

This collage depicts a semi-nude female figure, portrayed in a sardonic, derogatory manner. Her arms are outstretched above her head, and her brassiere dangles seductively from her right hand.

Pop Art

ROY LICHTENSTEIN (1923–97)

WHAAM!

LICHTENSTEIN'S work focused on issues confronting modern middle-class American life, in a culture that was just beginning to feel the effects of the mass media. Born in New York City, he pioneered his hallmark pastiches of comic strips in the early 1960s. Although his work parodied contemporary culture, it also cleverly paid homage to it.

In enormous close-up frames of brash, bold colors, he reduced simple subject matter to strongly stylized patterns of graphic inventiveness, including cartoon speech balloons and exclamations such as *Whaam!* (1963). He composed the pictures from minute circles, carefully reproducing the dots associated with the cheap screen-printing techniques of highly popular comic and newspaper strips. His subject matter often included the glamorized all-action heroes and blonde heroines of comic-strip cartoons.

Lichtenstein's Pop Art, with its pioneering and sardonic tones, calls upon the influence of artist Richard Hamilton. This work has been fantastically and innovatively constructed. The artist also produced sculptures, as well as a stunning five-storey mural for the lobby of the Equitable Life Assurance building in New York.

Pop Art

ROBERT RAUSCHENBERG (1925–)

RESERVOIR

BORN in Texas, Robert Rauschenberg studied in Kansas and at the prestigious Académie Julian in Paris. He was originally inspired by the work of the Dada and Surrealist schools before becoming associated with Jasper Johns, whose work was seen as a definite link between Abstract Expressionism and Post-modernism and Pop Art.

Rauschenberg was a trail-blazer of the 1960s notion that anything could constitute art material, and that by harnessing the environment our perceptions of life could be challenged. Now known as "combines" or process art, his work is a random mixture of painting, collage, and readymades. His radical assemblages accordingly include industrial junk such as corrugated cardboard, boxes, and shipping labels—a feature that has been copied by many later installation artists.

His work often incorporates silk-screen prints and photographic images, as in *Reservoir*. Because the final appearance of a piece could alter, depending on its place of installation or due to the effects of time on the materials, he draws attention to art's temporality, questioning its presumed permanence. In doing so, he reemphasizes the process of construction, a trend that was begun by the Bauhaus kinetic constructions of Moholy-Nagy and later developed by Pollock and Beuys.

ANDY WARHOL (1928–87)

CAMPBELL'S SOUP

A CULT 1960s figure who was associated with the hippy drug culture and emerging punk movement, Andy Warhol is regarded as the chief protagonist of Pop Art. He was also a film-maker and the manager of the famous rock band The Velvet Underground. He worked as a commercial artist between 1949 and 1960 and, significantly, transferred these techniques into powerful parodies of consumerism and advertising.

Warhol was influenced by British artist Richard Hamilton, who pioneered Pop Art, and the Post-modernist sculptures of Jasper Johns. Borrowing materials from other media, Pop Art studied the emerging effects of a new global mass media on popular culture, and the subsequent creation of new universal icons such as Marilyn Monroe, J. F. Kennedy and Elvis Presley, all of whom were subjected to Warhol's treatment. His bohemian collective, "the Factory," won notoriety despite several of its members, including Post-modernist artist Jean-Michel Basquiat, dying from drug overdoses. His images, as in the *Campbell's Soup* screen print, are perhaps more famous than the original items, restating Post-modernist questions about the ownership of an image and the process of originality.

DAVID HOCKNEY (1937–)

PACIFIC COAST HIGHWAY AND SANTA MONICA

DAVID Hockney studied at the Royal College of Art in London between 1959 and 1962, winning international acclaim for his Pop Art and Modern Realist work. Heavily influenced by R. B. Kitaj (1932–), he moved to the US in the early 1960s, and is often referred to as the "official" painter of California. During the 1960s and early 1970s he recorded the hippy era in a series of celebrity double portraits.

Hockney spends much of his time in the creative isolation of his small house in Malibu Beach, California. He often likes to paint the ocean. "The waves come right up to my window. Once again I am aware of an enormous space. The house is small, with very comfortable rooms, and outside is infinity."

In *Pacific Coast Highway and Santa Monica* we see a fusion of all the naturally occurring colors and lighting of his adopted home. Hockney loved to experiment with new fabrics; this work is on colored and pressed paper pulp. His later experiments in the 1990s employed technological developments such as faxes and photocopiers.

Pop Art

VICTOR VASARELY (1908–97)

VEGA 200

VICTOR Vasarely was born in Hungary and studied at the Podolini-Volkmann Academy in Budapest. In 1928 he went on to the Budapest Bauhaus where he was influenced by the work of Josef Albers, and constructivists including Kandinsky and Malevich. In 1930 Vasarely moved to Paris, where he worked as a graphic artist.

Vasarely was the foremost leader of the Op Art movement. His vision marked a transformation in twentieth-century art. In 1947 he observed that "internal geometry" was to be seen under the surface of the whole world. Most famously it was Vasarely and Bridget Riley who dominated the innovation in color and visual illusion that emerged in the 1960s. For Vasarely and his fellow Op Artists, color and form were indivisible. Nature in its varied forms is reflected through geometric patterns in Vasarely's work. Long before computer graphics and other digitally produced art, Vasarely anticipated the synergy that technology could offer his work.

From 1968, Vasarely used the deformity of lines to develop his "universal structures" into a style that he called "Vega." In this development, he uses illusory swelling of the shapes to produce a visual deformity. The canvas emerges from a two-dimensional context into a three-dimensional image.

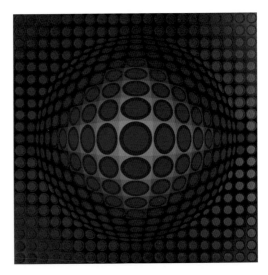

BRIDGET RILEY (1931–)

CURRENT

RILEY was one of the first notable successes produced by London's Goldsmith College, where she studied from 1949 to 1952 before entering the Royal College of Art. In the late 1950s she worked in advertising while privately exploring unusual color effects through dot paintings, in which the colors of an Italian landscape are apparently made to vibrate under the still heat of a Mediterranean summer.

Current belongs to Riley's four-year "black and white period" of the early 1960s, when she experimented with optical effects achieved through a mathematical distortion of parallel lines. The waving or moiré effect is extremely convincing as an illusion of movement. This work was iconic as a representation of the Op Art style.

These experimental abstracts by Riley were an instant success. In terms of school or tradition she is identified with Victor Vasarely (1908–97), who is considered the father of the art of optical illusion through the creation of abstract patterns: Op Art. Riley's work in this field is outstanding for its precision and polish, the result of careful calculation, experiment, and a fanatical approach to technique. It made Riley one of the new stars of the art world in 1960s London.

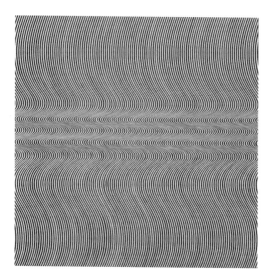

Op Art

EDWARD HOPPER (1882–1967)

ROOM IN BROOKLYN

HOPPER was almost certainly America's most important twentieth-century Realist painter. Born in New York state, he emerged in the late 1930s, bucking the trend of abstraction that was sweeping across Europe and the US. He studied at the New York School of Art (1900–06) under Robert Henri (1865–1929), the founder of the Philadelphia Realist group, and forged a purely American style, despite traveling in Europe between 1906–10. Hopper exhibited in Henri's celebrated 1913 New York Armory Show, which was the first exhibition of Post-impressionist and Cubist works in the US.

By 1913 a mood of melancholy pervaded his work, which intensified in later years. Paintings of empty streets, storefronts and solitary figures, often in urban settings, conjure an atmosphere of solitude and alienation. The stillness of the paintings is accentuated by their formality, combined with hard light and shadow and a focus on large, solid masses of architecture.

This despondency is clearly evident in this piece. The woman, sitting with her back to us, and her head held down to her chest, in an empty room, conveys a mood of solitude. The oppressive buildings outside the window accentuate this feeling.

Modern Realist

YASUO KUNIYOSHI (1889-1953)

THE ORIENTAL GIFT

THIS multi-talented Japanese-American artist was fluent in collage, textiles, and painting. Kuniyoshi was a social realist who used clear geometric forms set against unrealistic perspectives. His painting could be at times clear and fluid or at other times, thick with dense strokes and soft edges. He was fond of including circus performers in his works. In New York, he had studied under Robert Henri at the National Academy of Design, and with Kenneth Hayes Miller, at the Art Students League. Kuniyoshi traveled to Europe in 1925 and settled in Paris for a while, studying lithography.

Following a brief return to Japan in 1931, he worked in the US WPA's arts project. This came at the onset of the Great Depression. He flirted briefly with Surrealism. Paintings such as *Fisherman* (1924) show both his interest in and a blend of his two cultures. In the years following the Second World War, Kuniyoshi began to incorporate a range of brilliant colors including rich golds and purples. He worked within his medium in a reverential manner that was richly infused with primitive myths and symbolism.

The Blue Rider and Expressionist schools influenced his earliest works. Kuniyoshi was also an advocate of photographic experimentation. His work from the 1920s displays a unique synthesis of oriental and Modern Expressionist influences. Kuniyoshi's figurative subjects were often very flat and one-dimensional.

Modern Realist

FRANCIS BACON (1909–92)

STUDY AFTER POPE INNOCENT X BY VELÁZQUEZ

Aberdeen Art Gallery and Museum © DACS 2003; Francis Bacon/Celimage.sa/Scala Archives

BORN in Dublin of British parents, Bacon traveled extensively throughout Europe. He eventually settled in London, where he worked as an interior designer before taking up fine art.

Despite having no formal art training, he rose to become a central figure of the international Realist scene, and his often penetrating, disturbing, and perverse visions of the human form had a profound effect on the development of nude studies.

Bacon admired van Gogh's ability to capture raw emotion in his paintings, and was inspired to create a series of similar works in which his previously subdued palette exploded in a bruisingly violent use of color. He was also fascinated by Old Masters Goya and Velázquez, adapting his famous study after Velázquez's portrait of Pope Innocent X (1650) into a shocking series that incorporated X-ray visions, legs of meat, and screaming faces. He often worked when drunk; his figures are a balance between chance and order, constrained by the shape of the canvas but melting into a mire of oozing color.

RAYMOND MASON (1922–)

ALTARPIECE FOR SAINTE-EUSTACHE

Church of Sainte-Eustache, Paris © DACS 2003; Raymond Mason/Celimage.sa/Lessing Archive

STANDING near the beginning of the rue Montorgueil in Paris is the renowned church of Sainte-Eustache. This beautiful gothic renaissance church, is modeled on Notre Dame Cathedral. Since 1637 this was the church of the merchants of Paris and stood as a testament to the prosperity of the adjacent Les Halles area and its market. Cardinal Richelieu, Molière, and Mme de Pompadour were all baptized in Sainte-Eustache. Louis XIV received communion in its sanctuary, and Mozart held his mother's funeral there. This church is named after Sainte-Eustache, a Roman general who adopted Christianity. As punishment for converting, the Roman authorities imprisoned him in a brass bull that was then placed over a fire.

In a side chapel near the front of the church is a clay sculpture, created by Raymond Mason in 1969. This humorous work depicts a procession of grieving merchants who are heavily laden with fruit and vegetables. They are leaving their beloved market at Les Halles. In this unusual work, Mason emotionally conveys the intensity of human expressions. The relief is ominously colored in heavy dark tones. Movement is implied as the figures heave from left to right against a crowded city background.

Raymond Mason is an English sculptor based in Paris since 1946. He trained at the Birmingham School of Arts and Crafts. His works are to be found around the world with many sited in North America.

Modern Realist

ARIK BRAUER (1929–)

THE WIND MAGICIAN

ARIK Brauer was born in Vienna in 1929. He is a multi-talented and diverse artist, printmaker, stage designer, and singer. From 1945 to 1951 Brauer studied under Albert Gütersloh at the Akademie der Bildenden Künste in Vienna.

Brauer developed an increasing interest in oriental and Islamic styles, and used strong vibrant colors in his work. He placed Jewish and Old Testament themes at the heart of his paintings.

The Wind Magician is a dark and ominous work. The center of the painting is dominated by an enigmatic figure, whose face has an expression of contentment. The figure is surrounded by symbolic elements such as birds. The overall impression is of desolation and cold, a hostile environment within which this solitary figure dominates.

The objects within the painting are portrayed with an admirable realism, and yet their color and background setting are completely unreal. There is a great imbalance between the bright and dark colors across the painting, almost as if two worlds or images are being mistakenly overlapped.

RACHEL WHITEREAD (1963–)

WATERTOWER

LONDON-BORN artist Rachel Whiteread is one of art collector Charles Saatchi's most famous protégées. She won international acclaim for her sculptural work, in which familiar objects are irreverently cast in life-size forms as monuments to everyday life. In *Ghost* (1990), a whole room from a Victorian house was cast in plaster, with its contours turned inside out in the manner of a photographic negative image, leaving fossil-like traces of the windows, mantelpiece, and door.

Whiteread then moved on to cast a derelict house in concrete on its original site in the East End of London. Its features were turned inside out to create another bizarre "negative" of the entire building, which took on the appearance of a massive sarcophagus to memory, time, and life; it was as though time and space were suspended in concrete. *House* won the prestigious Turner Prize in 1993 but, despite much protest, the building was demolished by the local authorities three months later.

Her ingenious works challenge our fixed notions of time and space, and force us to re-evaluate art's traditional handling of such concepts.

Modern Realist

ABSTRACT EXPRESSIONIST An American movement of the 1940s and 1950s, its most famous proponents were Pollock, de Kooning, and Rothko. With roots in Surrealism, it attempted to break from Europe and tradition.

ANCIENT ART Premodern art often favored drawing over color. Much surviving work was recently discovered in tombs, such as Egyptian frescoes, pottery and metalwork.

ART NOUVEAU A European and American applied art movement of the late nineteenth and early twentieth century. It is characterized by sinuous lines and stylized natural forms. Famous artists include Gaudí, Mucha, and Charles Rennie Mackintosh.

BAROQUE A style of art and architecture that flourished in Europe from the late sixteenth to the early eighteenth century. This highly ornamented style was concerned with balance and harmony of the work.

BAUHAUS German school founded in 1919 to raise the profile of crafts to that of the fine arts. It established a relationship between design and industry and influenced the teaching of art.

BLOOMSBURY GROUP Meeting in the Bloomsbury area of London in the early twentieth century, this group of artists and writers was an intellectual elite reacting against the restrictions of Victorian Britain.

BYZANTINE Religious art relating to this eastern Roman Empire established in the fourth century, characterized by massive domes, rounded arches, and mosaics.

CLASSICAL ART Relating to or in the form of ancient Roman and Greek art and architecture. Primarily concerned with geometry and symmetry rather than individual expression.

CUBIST An abstract form of art, developed in Europe in the 1900s by Picasso and Braque. It abandoned realistic representation of perspective and subject and concentrated on solidity and volume.

EARLY MEDIEVAL A highly religious art from the period beginning in the fifth century in western Europe. Characterized by iconography and paintings illustrating scenes from the Bible.

EARLY RENAISSANCE Beginning in the fourteenth century in Italy, this period attempted to emulate Classical art's concern with symmetry and naturalism, searching for the perfect form.

EXPRESSIONIST Movement of the early twentieth century that concentrated on painting emotions instead of physical reality. Bright colors and strange forms are typical in such works.

FAUVIST From the French for "wild beast," this early-twentieth-century style is characterized by strong colors and expressive brushwork which convey an emotional and fantastical depth.

FLEMISH BAROQUE Spain and Catholicism influenced seventeenth-century Flanders, producing works that focused on spirituality and play of light, yet were still sensuous and colorful.

HIGH RENAISSANCE Developing from the early Renaissance in the fifteenth century, Italian artists such as Michelangelo and Titian were interested in perspective and the illusion of space. They created more realistic pictures than ever before.

IMPRESSIONIST Named after Monet's depiction of the effect of light on the French countryside in the 1860s, this group of artists was concerned with representing contemporary experience rather than historical events or the imagination.

INTERNATIONAL GOTHIC This amalgamation of northern European and Italian styles was fashionable in the late fourteenth century and is characterized by elegance and an interest in detail.

MANNERIST A reaction against the harmony and order of sixteenth-century art, typified by elongated forms and dramatic movement.

MODERN REALIST This late-twentieth-century American and British movement was influenced by consumerism, often reproducing photograph-like techniques of everyday scenes.in a glamorous way.

NABIS Inspired by Gauguin's use of color, this group of Parisian artists was active in the 1890s. They were unconcerned with depicting reality, preferring the emotional use of color and distortion.

NEOCLASSICAL Influenced by the Classical concern with symmetry and order and the eighteenth century's fascination with science, this European movement was fashionable during the Enlightenment.

NORTHERN LANDSCAPE Paintings of northern European countryside on a large scale, in particular the Netherlands and Germany. This genre was most popular in the sixteenth century.

NORTHERN RENAISSANCE From the sixteenth century, the Netherlands and Germany were influenced by Italy but the "rebirth" of their art was concerned with religious reform and old Christian values.

POP ART A movement of the 1950s inspired by advertising and consumer society. Artists such as Andy Warhol and Richard Hamilton produced works reminiscent of comics and advertising.

POST-IMPRESSIONIST A late-nineteenth-century reaction to Impressionism, this group explored a symbolic use of strong colors and form rather than concerning itself with naturalism.

Post-modernist Late-twentieth-century artists challenged traditional notions of what art actually is with a variety of different works; they are always experimental and innovative.

Pre-Raphaelite A British artistic group formed in 1848 that emulated Renaissance painters. The subject matter was often historical or literary, and concerned itself with morality.

Realist Art that attempts to represent the world in an accurate or familiar way. Everyday scenes are favored over idealized, historical, or mythological subjects.

Rococo This eighteenth-century style is highly decorative and ornamental. The palette was often pastel and the subjects were playful and erotic.

Romantic An American and European movement of the late eighteenth century.

The works were idealized and emotional rather than intellectual, laying importance on individual experience and expression.

Spanish Baroque The seventeenth-century Inquisition influenced Spanish art, encouraging devotional works. Mythology and still life were also popular but painted in a dark palette.

Surrealist Dadaists were disillusioned and reacted against the destruction of the First World War, creating absurd anti-art. Surrealism developed from this in 1924, representing dreams and pure thought inspired by the writing of Freud.

Symbolist Interested in dreamscapes and emotional, often exotic, scenes, this late-nineteenth-century movement was inspired by literature. The works often use color and line to suggest and evoke.

ANNUNCIATION The moment when the angel Gabriel told Mary she was to have a son, frequently depicted in Gothic, Renaissance and Counter-Reformation art.

CHIAROSCURO The contrasting effects of light and shade, employed by artists such as Leonardo and Rembrandt.

CONTRAPPOSTO The twisting torso of a figure placing most of its weight on one leg, much favored by Renaissance artists.

FÊTES GALANTES Baroque and Rococo depiction of charming pastoral scenes, often in a pastel palette.

FORESHORTENING A technique that makes an object appear shorter and narrower as it recedes.

FRESCO A technique dating back to ancient Egypt, it involves applying pigment and water to a layer of wet plaster —*buon fresco*. When applied to dry plaster it is *fresco secco*.

GENRE PAINTING Most common in Holland in the seventeenth century, these paintings depict scenes of everyday life.

IMPASTO Thickly applied opaque paint which retains the brush marks.

MAESTÀ Meaning "majesty," it describes paintings and altarpieces of the Virgin and Child surrounded by saints and angels.

MOSAIC Created by the Romans, this technique involves making images by assembling colored pieces of glass and stone in cement on floors or walls.

PIETÀ Italian for "pity": artworks representing the Madonna with the dead Christ in her arms.

SACRA CONVERSAZIONE "Holy conversation," a representation of the Virgin and Child with saints in a separate scene. Popular in Renaissance Italy.

SOTTO IN SÙ Meaning "below upward," this technique is usually associated with Baroque art. Extreme foreshortening on ceiling decoration creates the illusion of floating figures in the space above the viewer's head.

TEMPERA The most important technique for panel painting in thirteenth-century Europe until oil painting was introduced. It involved mixing pigment with water and glue.

TRIPTYCH Three pictures or carvings hinged together to fold and protect the central image and ease carrying.

TROMPE–L'OEIL French for "deceive the eye," details or paintings that have been created to trick the viewer into thinking the image is real.

VIGNETTE An image that has no clear border, allowing it to fade into the background.

INDEX OF ARTISTS

Index of Artists